DISCOVERING
The
Holy Spirit

Who the Holy Spirit Is and How He Is at Work
in Our Lives Today.

Hermie Reynolds

Discovering the Holy Spirit
Copyright © 2015 by Hermie Reynolds

All rights reserved. No part of this book may be reproduced, stored in a retrieval system, or transmitted in any form or by any means-electronic, mechanical, photocopy, recording, or otherwise-without prior written permission of the copyright owner.

Unless otherwise identified, Scripture quotations are taken from the New King James Version. Copyright © 1982 by Thomas Nelson, Inc. Used by permission. All rights reserved.

Scripture quotations marked AMP are taken from the Amplified® Bible, Copyright © 1954, 1958, 1962, 1964, 1965, 1987 by The Lockman Foundation. Used by permission.

Scripture quotations marked NLT are taken from the Holy Bible, New Living Translation, copyright 1996, 2004. Used by permission of Tyndale House Publishers., Wheaton, Illinois 60189. All rights reserved.

Scripture quotations marked MSG are taken from *THE MESSAGE*. Copyright © by Eugene H. Petersen 1993, 1994, 1995, 1996, 2000, 2001, 2002. Used by permission of NavPress Publishing Group.

Scripture quotations marked TLB are taken from The Living Bible; Tyndale House, 1997, © 1971 by Tyndale House Publishers, Inc. Used by permission. All rights reserved.

ISBN: 978-0-9981529-4-3

Dedication

This book is dedicated to You, Holy Spirit, who has worked so faithfully in my life. You stirred my heart and introduced me to Jesus. In this journey You have never left me in the dust. You picked me up every time, encouraging me, helping me, teaching and showing me the right way to go.

Thank you to all the teachers, books, and friends who have taught me to hear God's voice and taught me about the Holy Spirit. I am very thankful for all the teaching and people God has brought into my life, always at the right time. I consider everything that I have learned very valuable and pray, Holy Spirit, that You will pour out the blessings that I have received in getting to know You and walking with You on others.

I dedicate this book to my family and many friends who have journeyed with me in writing the books. Thank you to my wonderful husband, John, for supporting me in writing and being a strength and support in my life. Thank you for truly loving Jesus; that is the biggest blessing a woman can ask for. Thank you to all my friends who have prayed for me and often encouraged me through very timely words. Eternity will reveal the result of your obedience.

Thank you to Andy and Cathy Sanders and 5 Fold Media for helping me to get this book published. May God bless you abundantly!

Endorsements

This third book of this three-part series is perhaps the most needed in this hour of our history. *Discovering the Holy Spirit* will help you learn more about Him. It will also help you connect with the third person of the Trinity in ways that you may have never thought of or ever actually done before. This One, the Holy Spirit, who was promised by the Lord Jesus Christ to come upon His disciples in power came to them on the day of Pentecost and set like fire upon them. The Spirit ignited His church to go forth and testify about Jesus throughout the four corners of the earth in great signs and wonders, miracles, healings, preaching, and more—for the glory and testimony of Jesus Christ. We need to learn and connect more with the Holy Spirit, and Hermie's book is a great tool to help you do just that. As the day of the Lord approaches, it is the work of the Holy Spirit to make ready the church for Jesus' return. I believe Hermie's book will be an instrument that the Spirit will use to help make you ready for the coming of our Bridegroom King, the Lord Jesus Christ.

Walter P. Barr
Director and Lead Pastor of the Cincinnati House of Prayer (C-HOP)

The Holy Spirit! The Bible refers to Him with many names: Counselor, Comforter, the Helper, the Spirit of wisdom and revelation, to name a few. Jesus said in John 14:26, "But the Helper, the Holy Spirit, whom the Father will send in My name, He will teach you all things, and bring to your remembrance all things that I said to you." Thanks be to the Lord for His ever present Holy Spirit! In her third book, *Discovering the Holy Spirit*, Hermie Reynolds explains how to see the "teaching" of the Holy Spirit in our everyday lives. This is a great handbook on who the Holy Spirit is, how He works today, and His relationship with us. I would highly suggest adding it to your personal library or giving it to a friend.

Jeff Maglich
Copastor, Oxford Vineyard Church

It is an honor and blessing to intercede for Hermie as she sets herself before the Lord and pours forth her love for Him and His people through her writing and in other ways. Along with countless others from across the earth, my mind and heart have been touched through Hermie's earlier books, *Discovering God* and *Discovering Jesus*. I have, however, awaited the writing and publishing of *Discovering the Holy Spirit* most of all. Often misunderstood and not fully embraced, we have much more to discover about and through this third person of the Trinity when we welcome Him fully into our lives to counsel, teach, equip, empower us moment by moment and day by day. May the Spirit reveal truth to you through the Scriptures that Hermie has been led to bring before us in this book. And may we each be encouraged through Hermie's personal witness, realizing that His active work in Hermie's life is (or can be) our witness in life as well.

John Gordon
Associate director and pastor, Cincinnati House of Prayer

It has been said that a communicator can take something very complex and make it simple. Hermie is definitely a communicator. She took something that could have been difficult and made it easy to understand. She is generous to share her family's experiences of the Holy Spirit so He is easier for us to recognize and respond to as we encounter the Holy Spirit.

Even as I read *Discovering the Holy Spirit*, I encountered Him. I read a prayer that I shared with a friend because it was quickened to me. As I read a Scripture quoted here, I realized it was for my friend so I immediately texted it to her. It was just right and she was abundantly blessed by it. Read this book and as you read, look and expect the Holy Spirit to speak in some way to you! Come, Holy Spirit!

Susan Courtney
Facilitator for Regional Prophetic Intercessors
Cincinnati, Ohio

Would you like to have a friend who is closer than a brother? A friend who knows what will happen before it happens? A friend who knows what to do in every circumstance? A friend who is not manipulative or controlling? Would you like a true friend who is always waiting to sit and talk with you, who will never abandon you? Most of us would answer "Yes!" to that question in a heartbeat. Read *Discovering the Holy Spirit* and learn just how present and accessible this kind of friend is to those who believe in Jesus Christ. This friend is the Holy Spirit.

Hermie Reynolds—student of Scripture, author, prayer leader, and anointed prayer warrior—takes us through the Bible to help us better understand the Holy Spirit, the least understood person of the Trinity. Using Scripture as well as her own life experience, Reynolds shows us that Jesus freely gives the gift of the Holy Spirit to all who profess Him as Lord and Savior and repent of their sins. Those sins are then "deleted" and the Holy Spirit comes to live within us as Friend, Helper, and Comforter, bringing power, discernment, and spiritual transformation into our lives.

This third book in the *Discovering God* series, *Discovering the Holy Spirit* is a must-read for all who seek to grow in their faith. As Reynolds writes, "We see the Holy Spirit where the action takes place." This action is not limited to the biblical figures who were filled with the Spirit. Just as Jesus operated in the power of the Holy Spirit, so can we, today, live victorious lives by not only getting to know, but by spending time on a daily basis with the Holy Spirit.

Kathleen Deyer Bolduc
Award-winning author of several books on disability and faith, including *The Spiritual Art of Raising Children with Disabilities* and *Autism & Alleluias*.

Hermie has a flowing writing style and she weaves some of her own life into her teachings along with Scripture. She shares a good foundation about the Holy Spirit and how He worked in Bible times and also in our personal lives today. Hermie includes helpful questions at the end of each section so the book is easily used for small group studies. I recommend this book for hungry Christians who are eager to grow in their relationship with God and want to know more about Him through the Holy Spirit.

Sandy Warner
Author of The Quickened Word @ www.thequickenedword.com

Contents

Foreword	11
Introduction	15
How to Use This Book for Group Discussion	17
Chapter 1: Welcome, Holy Spirit!	19
Chapter 2: Where Is the Holy Spirit in the Old Testament?	35
Chapter 3: Did Jesus Have the Holy Spirit?	51
Chapter 4: How Does the Holy Spirit Work in Me?	63
Chapter 5: The Holy Spirit Is My Helper	77
Chapter 6: The Holy Spirit Has a Ministry for Everyone	95
Chapter 7: The Holy Spirit Releases Training and Equipping Gifts	113
Chapter 8: Can I Receive the Gifts of the Spirit?	131
Chapter 9: How Do I Walk in the Fruit of the Spirit?	151
Chapter 10: How Do I Hear the Holy Spirit?	167
Chapter 11: Walking in the Fullness of the Holy Spirit	181
Chapter 12: Growing in the Holy Spirit	197

Foreword

The Reynolds family came to the United States in 1999, a real journey of faith for a young family of six. They pulled up stakes and resettled in North America, where at least the language was the same—well, sort of. Their daily dependence and pursuit of God was of a different quality than many people I met, or so it seemed to me. I met them a number of years later at local conferences and church services, and they always stood out as people with an abiding life in God.

In years to come, Hermie joined the Cincinnati House of Prayer, a prayer ministry that I led at the time. It was in this context that we became better acquainted. I loved to hear her pray, not just for the richness of her South African accent, but because she flowed from a secret history in God. One only arrives at such familiarity after years of cultivation. She seemed to reference the goodness of God in every conversation, always giving credit to the work of the Holy Spirit in her life.

I listen for pithy phrases like that; they signal spiritual life to me. They resonate with my own journey with the Spirit of God. Whenever I see that life, I always want to glean from what they've experienced. Hermie has packed a lifetime of learning into this last volume, *Discovering the Holy Spirit*. There is gold to discover for the hungry heart.

Many people know very little about the Holy Spirit, even if they've grown up in a Christian environment. They speak about Him but rarely talk to Him. It's as if He is standing outside the door of their experience, looking through a window and listening, but never asked for His thoughts.

Discovering the Holy Spirit

Growing in the Lord during my teen years, I hungered to live like Jesus lived. All throughout the New Testament I read of the amazing things that happened around Jesus. The blind received their sight, the lame walked again, demonic spirits were driven out, the dead were raised, jaw-dropping wisdom was heard. I was hungry to have the power of God's Spirit flow through me, just as Jesus promised, but I didn't really understand who the Holy Spirit was and how He worked.

This hunger eventually culminated into a prayer that went something like this: "God, there's got to be something more to this Christian life than what I'm experiencing right now. Why would You give me a hunger for more if You weren't able to fill it?" It was a question that grew into passionate prayer. I knew that Jesus said, "Blessed are those who hunger and thirst for righteousness, for they shall be filled" (Matthew 5:6)

Perhaps you have a similar prayer resounding in you.

Late one evening, as a college freshman, I prayed before falling off to sleep. I prayed again, "There's got to be more..." That night, however, something changed. I don't know why it was different that night, but no sooner had that prayer left my lips than I began to sense the presence of the Holy Spirit filling the room. Inexplicable joy welled up on my inside as I began to weep and laugh at the same time. I was filled with spontaneous worship and sang out to God. Praise seemed to roll forth from an inexhaustible source. It was then that I heard the voice of the Lord speak to my spirit, saying, "I have now come." It was a convincing moment that has informed my life ever since. The Holy Spirit is God on the earth and longs for relationship with us.

Much of the church has somehow lost this reality along the way. Never have people been so hungry for truth, so desperate for something more, so willing to do anything to fill the emptiness, yet remained so unfulfilled. We were created for God, to hunger for Him, and He is the only One who can satisfy that longing. The perfect answer for perfected hunger is God Himself. We were created to be filled with His Spirit. The Holy Spirit is God on the earth, and His dwelling place is in our spirit. It's time to get to know Him.

Hermie Reynolds

This book will open some doors for those looking to interact with the Holy Spirit. It will give tools for engaging with the third person of the Trinity. For others it will personalize your relationship with God. I pray that everyone who reads this book will no longer talk about the Holy Spirit, but actually speak with Him.

Go for it! The best is yet to come.

Rusty Geverdt
Missionary, pastor, and founder of Cincinnati House of Prayer

Introduction

The Holy Spirit or Holy Ghost is the least known person of the triune God. People easily get funny ideas about who He is and what He does, especially if they hear the word *ghost*. It is true He cannot be seen, but He is the One of whom Jesus said He would send a Helper, the Holy Spirit. This Helper was not only sent to the disciples. He is here to help us too.

It is easier to form a picture of Jesus. We can picture Him as a man walking the earth, healing people. He called God Father, and taught His disciples to pray, "Our Father in heaven" (Matthew 6:9). We can see God as a Father, Jesus a brother type of figure, but what about the Holy Spirit? When Jesus was baptized the Holy Spirit descended upon Him like a dove; as a child that was probably my inner picture of the Holy Spirit (Matthew 3:16).

There is so much more that we can learn from the Bible about the third person of the Trinity, the Holy Spirit. He is doing a very important work in people's hearts on earth today. He is a person and not a force. His feelings can be hurt, and He can be grieved (Ephesians 4:30). A dove is a good symbol to depict Him, because doves easily fly off when they are not comfortable in a situation. The Holy Spirit is sensitive too; He is more active in places where He feels welcome. It doesn't take a whole lot to welcome Him—just a humble heart, eyes focused on Jesus, and saying, "You are welcome. Holy Spirit, come!"

The first twenty years of my life I hardly knew Him, although I am sure He was at work in my life even though I didn't know it. Then in my late twenties God started to raise me up in a teaching gift. I learned from Scripture that He is a Helper, a Teacher. He opens the Scriptures to me. He helps me to pray. It was good to learn from Scripture who He was; it formed a good foundation. I didn't base what I knew about the Holy Spirit on experience or what others told me; instead it was based upon Scripture. Once I knew the truth that He is here to help me and work in my life, it was easier to recognize when He was doing something or speaking to me.

As I was writing this book I saw that I was using many examples of situations that my husband and I walked through together. I hadn't planned it that way, but eventually saw that it was God's plan. My husband and I are such opposites. John is always level-headed, not easily moved, while I am much more sensitive and emotional. If I only wrote the book from my experience, people might think that they should hear God the same way I had. But examples from both John and my life cover a wider perspective. God has a unique plan for each of our lives and it will not look the same. We can learn from different people and learn how God works in each of us individually.

My prayer is that study will help to give you the biblical foundation of who the Holy Spirit, the third Person of the triune God is. As you learn more about Him, may you come to recognize how He works in your life and how He speaks to you.

O Holy Spirit, may everyone who reads this book grow in recognizing how You work in them and in the world around them. Open the Scriptures and bring revelation as they read. May they come to learn and grow in how You speak, lead, and guide them. May they learn to yield to You and follow You as you draw them into a deeper love for Jesus and our Father God. May they welcome You into every area of their lives. We need You to become more like Jesus, to be able to love others like Jesus does, and to have wisdom in every situation.

> "And I will ask the Father, and He will give you another Comforter (Counselor, Helper, Intercessor, Advocate, Strengthener, and Standby), that He may remain with you forever—the Spirit of Truth, Whom the world cannot receive (welcome, take to its heart), because it does not see Him or know and recognize Him. But you know and recognize Him, for He lives with you [constantly] and will be in you" (John 14:16-17 AMP).

How to Use This Book for Group Discussion

This book can be read by itself or it can be used as small group material. When used for a small group, read the chapter that will be discussed ahead of time. If you have questions or thoughts about a section, mark it and talk about it in your group. Here are some ideas for how you can structure your group time and some basic guidelines you may want to set for your group to help keep things orderly.

Ideas for Group Time (One hour long)

- Welcome everyone and open with prayer.
- Use the first fifteen minutes to share questions or thoughts people had about the chapter. If someone has many questions and the leader feels it will take all the group time to answer them, then schedule a different time to talk about them unless you can put a time limit on the discussion and it will benefit the whole group.
- Use the next fifteen to twenty minutes for discussion questions. The questions are focused on digging deeper into Scripture and applying what each person is learning about God in their own lives. The questions don't have to be answered ahead of time; that can be done in the group.
- Use the remaining time for prayer and personal ministry. If the group is big enough and there are Christians who know how to pray for others, then divide the group in smaller groups of two or three people to pray. If the group is less than ten people, the person who wants to receive prayer can be seated in the middle while the others in the group pray for them. Often with this kind of prayer, the Holy Spirit will give different people impressions or pictures or prayers to pray that are very specific and helpful to the person being prayed for.

Set Some Guidelines for Discussion

- Don't get into any argumentative discussions. If questions come up that will take up a lot of group time, schedule a different time to discuss it with the person. Be sensitive to what the Holy Spirit wants to do. The purpose of the study is to grow personally. The purpose of the study is to get to know Jesus and talk about how He wants to meet us in our everyday life.
- Don't rush through the Scriptures; ask the Holy Spirit what He wants to speak to each of you as you go through the Scriptures and discuss them. The questions also have practical life application.
- The leader of the group should decide how to minister to those who need prayer.

Chapter 1: Welcome, Holy Spirit!

"The grace of the Lord Jesus Christ, and the love of God, and the communion of the Holy Spirit be with you all. Amen" (2 Corinthians 13:14).

My life began in a smaller city in South Africa. I grew up in church, surrendered my life to Jesus in my early twenties, and continued to regularly attend church. It wasn't until my early thirties that I learned about the Holy Spirit. Getting to know Him changed my life. My Christian journey became more exciting, *What will God do next? What will He speak to me today?* It doesn't mean I didn't have struggles. I sometimes felt God took way too long to come and "fix" my broken life, but the Bible came alive to me and the Holy Spirit taught me one step at a time, one Scripture at a time. *Holy Spirit, You are welcome here! This book is about You! May everyone who reads it meet You in its pages!*

Growing up I heard of the Holy Spirit as part of the benediction or in a christening—Father, Son, and the Holy Spirit. Other than that He seemed to be a vague member of the Trinity.

I had no idea who God was. I knew He lived in heaven, but the image I had was one of a strict grandfather who wasn't very pleased with me. I read and heard how He moved in the lives of the people in the Bible, but there it seemed to stop. I wasn't sure whether He really cared about me. God had to take care of the whole world; would He even have time for me? It didn't feel like He was much involved in my life. But I had the longing that somehow He would love me and that He cared about me; maybe Jesus did?

As a child I had a desire to get to know God and I tried to connect to Him. My mom gave me a devotional that I read in the evenings and I prayed the Lord's Prayer, but I didn't feel like I had much of a connection with God. Most of the day, I didn't have time to think about God. In the evening the devotional focused me on a Scripture, but I didn't have a relationship with God and I didn't know how to have one. At the beginning of eighth grade it was discovered that I had potential as a track and cross country runner and athletics began to consume my life. One day my coach said: *Do you ever thank God for the talent He has given you?* I didn't. I felt convicted about that and tried to thank God after every race, but it didn't last long. It seemed like God wasn't very interested in me, so I kind of lost interest in Him.

The pressures of very competitive athletics and often training twice a day took its emotional toll. I became performance driven and found it hard to cope with the pressure to perform and fulfill the expectations people had. Looking back I can see that it would have been much easier for me if I had known Jesus and knew how to cast my cares upon God, trusting Him to help me with every race and even accepting it when I didn't do well. During my college years my appearance became very important to me. A year or two down that path, I realized this road was destructive. I knew I would end up with an eating disorder if I continued. I decided to take a better route and started to focus on healthier eating rather than dieting.

Things got worse. A long term relationship ended. I was heartbroken. My wounded heart mixed with my desire to know God and I thought of the perfect solution—I should become a nun! The only problem was I was in a church tradition that didn't have nuns. I needed Jesus and I didn't know where to find Him. My search led me to the Christian bookstore. Somewhere there should be an answer to help me get my life on a road that had more purpose. In the book I found I read the statement that God doesn't have grandchildren. It made me think—if my mom and dad were Christians and they were children of God, then I had a dilemma. I could not be a grandchild of God, but who was I?

God is involved in our lives even when we don't know Him. He will draw us into situations that will lead us to Him. This revelation set up the stage to surrender my life to Jesus. Around that time a friend invited me to a Bible study where I was confronted with the question: *Where is Jesus in your life?* I realized He is somewhere in the midst of all the things that occupy my time, but definitely not in the first place. I prayed and surrendered my life to Jesus and put Him in the first place in my life. I started to attend a different church denomination.

One afternoon God had a divine appointment for me. A tall, handsome man crossed my path. It didn't take him long to come to the decision he wanted to marry me. The next year we were married, and now twenty-eight years later, we have four wonderful children and one wonderful son-in-law. My husband and I faced challenges and difficulties through the years. Both of us are strong-willed and that can bring conflict. My husband read this chapter and reminded me that he often says that he is always right. Today we can laugh about it. The Holy Spirit had a lot of work to do in both of our lives. I know that our marriage would not be what it is if I hadn't met Jesus and learned about the Holy Spirit. God has brought my husband and me through, good, challenging, lean, busy, and wilderness years to a place where I can truly say that we are in the best years of our marriage.

Looking back through my life, I am so thankful to God for the journey He has taken me on. He is the God of second and third chances. When we turn to Him, He can turn any life around. I can see the way He drew me to Himself. He didn't leave me there, but continued the journey and helped me to lose my baggage of insecurity, fear, rejection, performance orientation, and so much more. He set me free to be happy to be the person He has created me to be and not to desire or try to be someone else. It didn't happen instantaneously; situations happened that would stir up my issues, but now I know that the Holy Spirit was there to bring restoration to my life. He is the God who gives beauty for ashes.

In the Beginning

Let's start our journey at the beginning of the Bible. We find the Holy Spirit already present at creation: "In the beginning God (prepared, formed, fashioned, and) created the heavens and the earth. The earth was without form and an empty waste, and darkness was upon the face of the very great deep. The Spirit of God was moving (hovering, brooding) over the face of the waters" (Genesis 1:1-2 AMP). We can think of God as the Master Architect of the earth. He is the One with the blueprints. Jesus is the Word. We find words in a book, telling a story. The story comes to life when it is acted in a play. Jesus and the Holy Spirit brought God's blueprint to life and the heavens and the earth were formed: "All things were created through Him and for Him" (Colossians 1:16). Hebrews tells us that God spoke in the past through the prophets, but now He is speaking to us through His Son, "whom He has appointed heir of all things, through whom also He made the worlds; who being the brightness of His glory and the express image of His person, and upholding all things by the word of His power" (Hebrews 1:2-3).

We see the Holy Spirit where the action takes place. He is the One moving, hovering, brooding over the earth, taking God's plan and working together with Jesus, the Word, bringing forth creation.

We know God is omnipresent, everywhere present on earth; the Holy Spirit is omnipresent too.

"The Holy Spirit is *part of the Trinity*. He is identified as an equal with the other persons in the Trinity (see Matthew 28:19; 2 Corinthians 13:14). He shares with Jesus and the Father in the mysterious relationship that eternally exists within the Godhead.

"Jesus described the kind of relationship that exists within the trinity with statements like *"I and My Father are one"* (John 10:30); *"Anyone who has seen me has seen the Father"* (John 14:9 NLT) and *"He who rejects Me rejects Him who sent Me"* (Luke 10:16).

"That same kind of unity exists between Jesus and the Spirit. Just as Jesus was sent by the Father to be a visible manifestation of the invisible God, so the Holy Spirit was sent by Jesus to perfectly manifest His presence in the lives of His people. Just as those who received Jesus also received the Father, so those who receive the Spirit receive Jesus.

"The Holy Spirit is the perfect manifestation of Jesus in the world today. That is why it does not detract from Jesus to talk about the Holy Spirit. The one who relates to the Spirit is relating to Jesus, so the more you develop your relationship with the Holy Spirit, the closer your walk with Jesus will be."[1]

When Jesus went to heaven He sent an intimate friend who would be with us, who is one with Him and His Father, and who knows exactly what God is thinking and doing in each of our lives. If we allow Him, He can be a friend who is closer than a brother. He is a friend who knows what will happen before it happens and He knows what to do in every circumstance. Yet, this friend is not manipulative or controlling. He is a true friend. Always waiting that we will talk to Him and ask: *What should I do, Holy Spirit? Would You share with me how the Father feels about this person or situation? This friend or situation is on my heart today, what should I pray for this person, Holy Spirit?* Business and the cares of this life, trials and challenges can move Him to the back room. The reason Jesus sent Him to us can be forgotten and neglected. I have learned He is here with me all the time—when I feel Him and when it feels like He is a thousand miles away. He doesn't want to take over my life. He is waiting for me to yield, ask, and willingly say, *I want to do it God's way and not my own.*

I have a relationship with God, my heavenly Father, and I have a relationship with Jesus. When I pray for the world or pray for others I usually talk to God, my Father, in the name of Jesus. Then there are times when I talk to Jesus or just spend time fellowshipping and focusing on Jesus. I know the Holy Spirit is with me all the time, just as God and Jesus, because they're omnipresent, but in the areas where the Holy Spirit is specifically at work, I say, "Holy Spirit, help me to pray. Holy Spirit, open the Word to me." The Holy Spirit doesn't focus the attention on Himself. He draws us to Jesus and God, but that doesn't mean we should ignore Him. He enjoys working with us when we acknowledge Him, follow Him, and obey His promptings, or listen when He speaks to us.

There are not many Scriptures where we find all three persons of the Trinity in one Scripture verse. One such Scripture is where John the Baptist baptized Jesus. We see Jesus in the water, God the Father

---

1. Robert Heidler, *Experiencing the Spirit, Developing a Living Relationship with the Holy Spirit*, (Chosen Books, a division of Baker Publishing Group, 1988), 39.

speaking from heaven, and the Holy Spirit descending upon Jesus. Then one day Jesus came to be baptized along with all the others. "When all the people were baptized, it came to pass that Jesus also was baptized; and while He prayed, the heaven was opened. And the Holy Spirit descended in bodily form like a dove upon Him, and a voice came from heaven which said, 'You are My beloved Son; in You I am well pleased'" (Luke 3:21-22).

When I pause for a moment and think about this, I realize what those watching must have felt. It was a moment when mankind saw the triune God interact and they just stood in awe of what was happening. If you ponder on what God is saying to Jesus, "You are my Beloved Son" and relate it to John 17:23 where Jesus said that just as much as God loves Him, God loves us, then God is saying this to each one of us. *You are My beloved child.* The New Living Translation describes this beautifully, *"May they experience such perfect unity that the world will know that you sent me and that you love them as much as you love me"* (John 17:23 NLT).

John described Jesus' baptism like this, *"I watched the Spirit, like a dove flying down out of the sky, making himself at home in him"* (John 1:32 MSG). God told John the Baptist that the One he baptized on whom the Spirit of God descended will be the One who will baptize people with the Holy Spirit. John saw this word unfold right before his eyes. After His baptism, the Holy Spirit led Jesus into the desert for forty days where He was tempted by the Devil. Jesus came out of the desert in power. He went forth teaching with authority (Luke 4:32), doing miracles and healing people everywhere He went (Matthew 4:23-25). If Jesus needed an infilling of the Holy Spirit and the Holy Spirit resting upon Him, how much more do we need God's Holy Spirit!

What did Jesus say about the Holy Spirit?

Jesus knew when His time on earth was drawing near. He prepared His disciples. He told them that He was going to leave them and said that He was going to prepare a place for them and that when everything was ready He would come back for them. Thomas replied that they did not know where He was going and how to get there. Jesus was speaking about spiritual things and Thomas was thinking of a natural road. Jesus answered *"I am the way, the truth, and the life. No one comes to the Father except through Me"* (John 14:6). Thomas was thinking, *How do I get there?* And Jesus told him, *I am the way; you get there through Me.* Everyone who comes to belief in Jesus—that He died for their sins—and receives Jesus as their Savior goes through the gate to eternal life. Jesus is the gate (John 10:9).

Before Jesus went to the cross He shared with His disciples that He would be leaving them (John 16:28-32). He told them He would not leave them by themselves. He would ask His Father to send them a Helper. This Helper had been with them, but the time would come when He would live inside of them: *"But you know him, because he lives with you now and later will be in you"* (John 14:17 NLT) There is so much in John 14 that we can pause and consider. The Holy Spirit is a Helper, just like a friend. He helps me to love Jesus. He will come and live inside me. I can know Him intimately. Thank You, Jesus, for not leaving us by ourselves but asking our Father God to send the Holy Spirit to us.

When I opened my heart to Jesus, He and the Holy Spirit came into my life. A few years into this journey I went to a Bible study where a pastor taught about the Holy Spirit. It was very helpful to learn from Scripture first who the Holy Spirit was. It stirred a desire in me to walk more closely with Him and hear His voice and allow Him to be my friend. In the beginning of my Christian walk I only allowed Jesus in the living room of my spiritual house. Our spiritual house refers to our inner selves. It can be likened to a real house with rooms for the different functions in our lives. The Holy Spirit is the One who helped me on the journey to clean up my spiritual house. Think of the kitchen as symbolic of the place where we work. He showed me I get overwhelmed when I don't allow myself time to take a break or rest. At that time I was a mom with four little kids and had very little time to rest. It is not in the best interest of my family when I am frustrated and impatient most of the time. One step at a time, the Holy Spirit helped me clean up the kitchen and move on to different rooms in my life.

As I learned that it was safe to trust the Holy Spirit, I gave Him more access to the rest of my life. Some of the things that He revealed were painful, but as a friend of mine said, what the Holy Spirit reveals, He will also heal. I knew that if it was a painful situation—one that appeared in the present and connected to the past—the Holy Spirit was opening it up because He wanted to bring restoration, healing, or correction. There is nothing that He doesn't know. He can tell the future before it happens (Psalm 139:1-5; Isaiah 46:10).

It brings freedom to me to know that God knows everything. It doesn't help to hide anything when I make a mistake; the best thing is to humbly confess, *I am sorry, Jesus; forgive me, cleanse my heart, and let's continue the journey.* When God saved me, He didn't do it because I was perfect. He did it because I needed a Savior. I needed help. I was not making the best decisions living life in my own strength and power, even though I tried hard to be successful.

The Holy Spirit is the One tugging on our hearts, drawing us to Jesus. The Bible says that God has put eternity in the human heart (Ecclesiastes 3:11). Every person's human spirit came from God and has an awareness and longing for God in some way. We might try to squelch that through humanistic or other teachings, but there is a "homing device" on the inside of every person and a longing deep down to know God. When I was a teenager I thought the longing on the inside of me was to find the one who would marry me. Today I know that the longing I felt back then was actually a longing to know God. The only context I could place it in was finding some person who would love me, so I thought of my future husband. No person will completely fulfill us, and no person was meant to fulfill us. If a person is not happy in themselves and grounded in their relationship with God, then it places a burden on our relationship and it will not last.

The Holy Spirit was the One who gave me the idea to go to the Christian bookstore and look for a book that could help me. He had been tugging on my heart since I was a child. I just didn't know that. I didn't know that the longing I felt was to come to know the One who created me. He is tugging on your heart and those around you. *Holy Spirit, open our eyes, that we will see where You are working.*

When we say no at first, He comes again and again, because He knows there is a desire in our hearts to know Him, although we might not recognize it at first. He knows we will go through many challenges and it will be difficult to go through life without knowing Him. He uses circumstances, people, books, dreams, movies, and many other things and situations to stir a hunger in our hearts to know truth and to know God.

The Holy Spirit speaks to us through the Bible as we read the Word. He can highlight a Scripture, or bring a Scripture reference to mind and speak to us through it. He can speak to us through our everyday Bible reading. At times when we went through challenges I remembered and read 1 Peter 5:7 about casting my cares upon God or Matthew 6:26-28 about His provision. When I read a verse and it feels like the Holy Spirit is highlighting it, I pause there for a little bit and wait to see what God wants to speak to me about it. Sometimes He wants to strengthen or encourage me or minister His peace. Other times I turned it into prayer.

One time I was at a meeting and they were praying for people. After I received prayer I was standing there with my eyes closed enjoying God's presence and John 17:3 came to mind, and I didn't know the verse. As soon as I got back to my seat, I looked it up. *"And this is eternal life, that they may know You, the only true God, and Jesus Christ whom You have sent"* I never forgot that experience and this Scripture. If God found this verse so important that He spoke the Scripture reference to me, then it is important to me.

The Holy Spirit has a unique way of communicating with each of us. Some people have a stronger auditory sense and when they hear Him, they hear words in the language they speak. Others are more visual and might see pictures or have dreams. Some people are more emotionally sensitive, and might say, *I feel the Holy Spirit is stirring my heart to send an encouraging note to this friend.* There are many other ways that He speaks to us too. Sometimes you suddenly see something and it makes an impression on you. This is actually God showing you something.

When we became empty nesters we went through a huge transition. My husband and I had a hard time to come into agreement about a situation. He suggested that we see a counselor. After seeing the counselor, we were driving home, talking about unity, when a car stopped next to us with the license plate "IN UNITY." We knew that the Holy Spirit was speaking to us, and that we needed to come into agreement about the situation. During that same time as I was sitting at the house of prayer I saw the Kentucky state flag hanging above my head. On it is written "United we stand, divided we fall." God spoke clearly and He helped my husband and I dissolve our differences and unite with one another.

The Holy Spirit is also the One who empowers us for ministry. Everywhere that people met Jesus He changed their lives, some through a word or the parables He shared. The people recognized that He taught with authority. His teaching was different. We find a prayer in Ephesians 3:16 for strengthening and being filled by the Holy Spirit, *"I ask him to strengthen you by his Spirit—not a brute strength but a glorious inner strength—that Christ will live in you as you open the door and invite him in. And I ask him that with both feet planted firmly on love, you'll be able to take in with all followers of Jesus the extravagant dimensions of Christ's love"* (MSG). That is the Holy Spirit—He gives us supernatural strength to go through situations that can be very difficult in the natural. I experienced this when my mom was very sick in the ICU. I didn't know I had the strength to go through such a difficult time, being calm and mostly feeling God's peace. The Holy Spirit strengthened me. The Holy Spirit is the One with divine might and explosive power. Where His power is released, something happens.

Hearing the Holy Spirit can be difficult. It was very challenging to hear Him when God was changing our direction. It felt like something needed to happen, but I wasn't sure what. Once we discerned what God was doing, we had to understand the time frame for the changes He wanted to bring. In 1997 the consulting business my husband was part of went through some trouble because of the economic climate in South Africa. During that same time our car was stolen. This was tough for us because we were trusting God to help us through this transition and now things got worse. *What is going on? What do You want us to do, Lord?*

One morning I woke up around 5 a.m. and had a vision of our family standing in this brand-new road. During that same week my husband read a Scripture that He felt the Holy Spirit highlighted to him. It was in Joshua 3:14-16. The priests were carrying the ark on their shoulders and when they stepped into the Jordan River, the water parted. John felt he should look overseas for a job. We looked at England, Australia, and the United States. It is not that easy to find a job in a different country. The immigration laws and visa requirements are very strict. We were a few months into this process, but still there was nothing. One day I was hanging laundry on an outside clothesline. I was talking to God and said, *Father, we can't wait until my husband is as old as Abraham before You do something. We really need You to do something.*

God brought us back to the Scripture John received in the beginning and He gave John more revelation about it. John felt that an act of faith was required from us. He had the sense from the Scripture saying *the priests stepped into the river* that he should go into the river too. He thought he should fly across the ocean and go for job interviews. We met a couple at our children's school who had just visited the U.S., and they gave us newspapers they had brought back from Cincinnati. John contacted some of the companies for job interviews. He made some appointments, booked a plane ticket and hotel. Now we knew that this was not the best way to do this, but we also knew God had a plan.

In October of 1998, John flew to Cincinnati. I still remember how he felt that first night in the United States. He was wondering whether he had made the right decision. In the middle of the night, he woke up with 2 Corinthians 5:7 in his mind *"For we walk by faith, not by sight."* He knew God was encouraging him to continue on this journey. In Cincinnati he received a job offer. He called me from the states and told me it was going to be our new home. I had never been out of Africa and had no idea what this new home looked like.

When John got back, the process of obtaining a work visa began. We had to sell our house and decide whether we were going to move our furniture overseas or start fresh. We decided to just sell and give away what couldn't fit in our luggage. I told my children that Jesus would give them toys again. It is not an easy thing for a child to part with their toys. We sold our house by December and moved into an apartment. By the end of April our visa was approved. I was so overwhelmed when I heard of the visa approval that when I picked up the kids from school I left our middle son behind. Halfway home I realized I didn't have all the kids with me! My son reminded me of this for the next three months, *"Mom, don't forget to pick me up."*

Our children all reacted differently to this move. Our youngest son was four years old at the time, and he asked me to buy him a baseball bat. In South Africa they play cricket and not baseball, but I found a plastic bat and ball in the store. Every day he brought the plastic ball and bat to me and asked me to throw it to him so he could practice, telling me, "Mommy, I'm practicing for America." Our middle son was six years old; he said he didn't want to move. When he realized the whole family was going, he decided he would go for one day. The oldest two could comprehend more and were okay.

Arriving in the states the younger children adapted more quickly to the change. Our oldest son prayed for months for his old school in South Africa, that God would provide the money to fix the pool. A few months into this I realized I'd better contact someone from the school to find out if they had fixed the pool; if not, he was never going to stop praying for that pool. Our daughter was eleven and she adjusted well, but she remembered our family the best and missed her grandparents a lot.

Through it all God had shown His faithfulness to us. I thought the way He would give back the children's toys was that we would have the money to buy them. I was wrong; we didn't have much extra money those first years of starting over. God connected us with wonderful families and some of them had kids the age of our older children who outgrew their toys and they passed them on to our younger boys. Above all I think my children learned that their happiness did not lie in earthly possessions. They always loved to play outside, go on adventures, and play with sticks and rocks and continued to do that. On our first Christmas in the United States, we woke up Christmas morning and saw that it had snowed! We had never experienced snow in South Africa. The kids were outside at 7:30 a.m. in their snowsuits. Nobody else was outside. I knew it was God's way of blessing us. That Christmas we were not with our family as usual, but the excitement of seeing snow and playing in the snow was a wonderful experience to the kids.

It is a huge sacrifice to leave one's extended family and move to a different country. We knew God was in it all and looking back I can see how He brought us here to learn. There is such a rich history in the Holy Spirit in the U.S., and we learned and grew by hearing messages and attending trainings, conferences, and churches that had great depth in the Spirit. Following God doesn't mean the road will always be comfortable or without questions, but it means we will never be alone. We have a friend and Helper, the Holy Spirit who is with us; we have a friend and brother in Jesus and His blood to cleanse us from sins; and we have a Father in heaven who watches over us.

If you look at our journey—I saw a vision. My husband got a Scripture. Someone gave me a word that big changes were coming. In the natural, our car was stolen and the economic decline stirred us to look for a solution elsewhere. We didn't hear the audible voice of God or have a whole lot to go on other than trust and faith. Looking back I am amazed at what God has done in our family; and though we still miss our relations in South Africa, we have seen them since we moved away, but we know God had a much better plan than what we knew. He surely knows best.

Discovering the Holy Spirit

Discussion Questions: Welcome, Holy Spirit!

1. Write a description of who you think the Holy Spirit is. At the end of the book you will answer this question again.

___

2. When John the Baptist baptized Jesus, he said, *"I watched the Spirit, like a dove flying down out of the sky, making himself at home in him"* (John 1:32 MSG). Discuss what differences you see in Jesus before the Holy Spirit descended upon Him at His baptism and after this happened.

___

3. Read John 16:13-14 and John 14:9-13. What do these Scriptures reveal about the Holy Spirit and Jesus?

___

4. "But you know and recognize Him, for He lives with you [constantly] and will be in you" (John 14:17 AMP). Are you aware that the Holy Spirit lives in you? Share an example of a time where you experienced the leading of the Holy Spirit. If you can't think of a time, pray and ask the Holy Spirit to help you know Him more.

_____
_____
_____
_____

5. Take some time to ponder this Scripture. Allow the Holy Spirit to speak to you or minister to you from it.

> "The grace of the Lord Jesus Christ, and the love of God, and the communion of the Holy Spirit be with you all" (2 Corinthians 13:14).

Chapter 2: Where Is the Holy Spirit in the Old Testament?

"But truly I am full of power by the Spirit of the Lord, and of justice and might" (Micah 3:8a).

We often find the word *Holy Spirit* or *Spirit* in the Bible in the places where God is working in and through people on the earth. The Holy Spirit works in people's lives to restore them back into relationship with God, *"No one can come to Me* (Jesus) *unless the Father who sent Me draws him"* (John 6:44). Although this verse mentions God, the Father, we see in John 16:8 that it is the Holy Spirit who convicts the world of sin. Jesus mentioned the Holy Spirit only a few times before John 16. In Luke 11:11-14 He told the people that God is a good Father and He will give them His Spirit if they ask Him.

In the Bible we read about people who didn't want to follow God and many others who obeyed Him. Even though they didn't do it perfectly, they set their hearts on a path of obeying and following God. They learned many lessons along the way and grew in their faith. In the Old Testament we read how God spoke to people and we often find different names for God connected to the revelation God gave the person. God revealed Himself as One God (Deuteronomy 6:4). You will find more information around this in the first book of this series, *Discovering God*. Whether it is God, Jesus, or the Holy Spirit speaking—the message is from God.

In Genesis 4:6-9 we find God talking to Cain. The word *Lord* is translated from *Yehovah*, which means "the existing One" and is the proper noun for God.[2] Cain became very angry that God didn't receive

---
2. Brown, Driver, Briggs, and Gesenius, "Hebrew Lexicon entry for *Yehovah*." The KJV Old Testament Hebrew Lexicon, accessed March 1, 2015, http://www.biblestudytools.com/lexicons/hebrew/kjv/yehovah.html.

his sacrifice. It could be because God required a blood sacrifice for the forgiveness of sins and Cain brought a grain sacrifice. God saw the anger in Cain's heart and reached out to him and warned him, *"'Why are you so angry?' the Lord asked Cain. 'Why do you look so dejected? You will be accepted if you do what is right. But if you refuse to do what is right, then watch out! Sin is crouching at the door, eager to control you. But you must subdue it and be its master'"* (Genesis 4:6-7 NLT).

Take notice—this incident happened after Adam and Eve were expelled from the garden of Eden. Here we find God talking to Cain after Adam and Eve sinned and lost their intimate relationship with Him. God didn't leave mankind alone. His involvement with people continued, although that ease of walking in a close relationship with God as a friend was lost. We see that it was possible for people to have a relationship with God after the fall during Old Testament times. Noah, Abraham, Moses, David, and others had a close relationship with God.

But Cain didn't listen to God's instruction, and the result was the first instance of murder in the Bible. He killed his brother, Abel. The Holy Spirit strives with men to try and get them to do the right thing. Before the flood people lived for hundreds of years. Methuselah lived the longest—969 years. The people became so evil that God decided, *"My Spirit shall not strive with man forever, for he is indeed flesh; yet his days shall be one hundred and twenty years"* (Genesis 6:3). The word for Spirit is the word *ruwach* in Hebrew, which refers to God's Spirit or the Holy Spirit.[3] The word *pneuma*[4] is the Greek Word used for Spirit that has the same meaning, referring to God's Spirit or the Holy Spirit. It is the same Holy Spirit who worked in both the Old Testament and the New Testament.

In Genesis 6:3 we read that God shortened the number of years that people would live to no longer than 120 years. God's Spirit didn't want

---

3. Ibid., "Hebrew Lexicon Entry for *ruwach*," The KJV Old Testament Hebrew Lexicon, accessed March 1, 2015, http://www.biblestudytools.com/lexicons/hebrew/kjv/ruwach-2.html.
4. Thayer and Smith, "Greek Lexicon entry for *pneuma*," The KJV New Testament Greek Lexicon, accessed March 1, 2015, http://www.biblestudytools.com/lexicons/greek/kjv/pneuma.html.

to "strive, contend, or plead"[5] with man for hundreds of years. In this passage we read that people became so evil, that *"the Lord was sorry he had ever made them and put them on the earth. It broke his heart"* (Genesis 6:6 NLT). They exchanged the ability to live in a trusting, intimate relationship with God for the knowledge of good and evil and wisdom; deciding and discerning for themselves was better than being dependent on God and trusting God that He knew best. Man's "wisdom" has led many down troublesome paths.

As a parent I can understand how God felt. There is nothing that hurts a parent more than when a child chooses the wrong path. Most parents have experienced life long enough that they have the insight that addictions to drugs and alcohol or sexual immorality leads to the destruction of a child's body, soul, and spirit. A parent has the child's best interest at heart. I am blessed when I know my children walk with God and are being blessed. It doesn't mean they don't have challenges, but when they make good choices I know it will produce good fruit in their lives. God's involvement in our lives is the same. He knows which choices will be best and the Holy Spirit works with our stubborn human hearts to bring us to a place of surrendering our own knowledge of good and evil to God's best plan.

As a mom I know how much effort it takes to raise kids. Many times I had to repeat the same thing over and over again before they got it. Years ago I went shopping with my oldest son, who was four years old at the time. I bought him a bag of potato chips. When he finished it, he threw the empty bag on the ground. I realized he didn't automatically know that he shouldn't throw trash on the ground. I had to teach him the reason why we don't do that. The streets will get very dirty if everybody leaves their trash on the ground. We take responsibility to help keep the city clean and throw our trash in the garbage can. Children need to be taught the right way of living, not with condemnation but in love; how else will they know the right thing to do?

---

5. Brown, Driver, Briggs, and Gesenius, "Hebrew Lexicon entry for *diyn*," The KJV Old Testament Hebrew Lexicon, accessed March 1, 2015, http://www.biblestudytools.com/lexicons/hebrew/kjv/diyn.html.

Discovering the Holy Spirit

When our daughter turned sixteen, she began to make her own choices and not just obey everything I told her to do. She wasn't making bad choices, but this was quite a shock to me. I didn't realize that soon my kids would come to the age when they would be independent and not always follow my advice. I thought I had a lot more time to teach them. I knew that little by little I needed to let go and help them become independent and able to make responsible decisions. God feels the same. It hurts Him and grieves His Spirit to see people make decisions that will hurt them and others. It also brings God great joy when a person surrenders his life to Jesus, surrenders his own will, and starts following and obeying His Word and His Spirit.

One of my favorite Bible characters is Joseph. We see God at work in his life. Joseph was Jacob's son by Rachel, his favorite wife. His father loved him more than his brothers and had a beautiful coat specially made for him. His brothers were envious of him, not only because he was the favorite, but because he told on his brothers and had outlandish dreams. One time Joseph dreamed they were tying up bundles of grain and the bundles of his brothers gathered around his bundle and bowed low before it. This didn't help the situation with his brothers at all (Genesis 37:5-8).

When Joseph was around seventeen years old, his dad asked him to take food to his brothers who were tending the sheep in Shechem. Joseph finally found his brothers in Dothan. When they saw him in the distance they plotted to kill him, "Come on, let's kill him and throw him into one of these cisterns. We can tell our father, 'A wild animal has eaten him.' Then we'll see what becomes of his dreams!" (Genesis 37:20 NLT). Reuben had compassion on Joseph and came to his rescue. He convinced his brothers to throw Joseph in an empty well instead as he was planning to later rescue Joseph.

Midianite traders came by and Judah's conscience was stirred too. He suggested that they sell Joseph. Joseph was sold to traders who took him to Egypt where he was sold as a slave. The brothers tore Joseph's coat, sprinkled it with blood, and sent it to their father with a message that a wild animal had killed Joseph. God had a plan for Joseph's life. It was the Holy Spirit who stirred Reuben and Judah's conscience not to kill

Joseph. Even in Egypt in the midst of an impossible situation, God took care of Joseph. Potiphar, an officer of Pharaoh, bought him. Potiphar soon noticed that God's favor rested upon Joseph—everything Joseph did prospered. He put Joseph in charge of his household. Potiphar's wife tried to seduce Joseph and when he refused her, she brought false accusations against him which landed him in prison. In Joseph's eyes this was unfair, but God had a plan.

God was with Joseph even in prison. "Before long, the warden put Joseph in charge of all the other prisoners and over everything that happened in the prison. The warden had no more worries, because Joseph took care of everything. The Lord was with him and caused everything he did to succeed" (Genesis 39:22-23 NLT). There's a clear difference between Joseph and Cain. Cain got offended and angry when God didn't receive his offering. Joseph was a bit prideful when he was a child, knowing he was his father's favorite, but as a slave in Egypt, Joseph still followed the beliefs that he was taught in his father's house. Even when he was sent to prison, he kept his heart pure and unoffended. God used all he experienced as preparation for Joseph's destiny.

When Pharaoh's cupbearer was in prison with Joseph, he had a dream which Joseph interpreted correctly. He forgot about Joseph after he was released from prison, but remembered him when Pharaoh had a dream that nobody could interpret. God's appointed time had come. The cupbearer told Pharaoh about Joseph and Pharaoh sent for him. Pharaoh asked Joseph to interpret his dream, "'It is beyond my power to do this,' Joseph replied. 'But God can tell you what it means and set you at ease'" (Genesis 41:16 NLT).

Joseph did not hide his faith in God. Pharaoh was considered a god and had the highest authority in Egypt. No man would risk his life to confess his dependence upon a different god than Pharaoh. Joseph's trust and faith in God was stronger than his fear of Pharaoh. He prayed and shared the dream interpretation with Pharaoh and the wisdom about what to do: "So Pharaoh asked his officials, 'Can we find anyone else like this man so obviously filled with the spirit of God?'" (Genesis 41:38 NLT). What a response coming from a man who was considered to be a god. He recognized this revelation and information was from a higher source. He could also see that God's presence and favor was upon Joseph's life.

Pharaoh promoted Joseph as second in command in Egypt. Joseph was promoted from being a prisoner to being a ruler in one day. It was God's plan to place Joseph in Egypt to save Joseph's family, Egypt, and the surrounding nations from famine. Joseph is an example of what God wants to do in and through Christians in the marketplace and government. We have the Holy Spirit in us, access to the God Most High. His wisdom is available to us if we ask when we pray, then listen and obey. Ordinary men and women will accomplish extraordinary tasks for God in the work that God has for them.

Joseph's dad, brothers, and the rest of the family moved to Egypt through God's miraculous intervention. They became a large nation and were eventually enslaved by the Egyptians. Working through Moses next, God released ten plagues on the Egyptians until Pharaoh finally let the Israelites go to serve God. They still celebrate God's deliverance out of Egypt as the Passover Feast (Genesis 39–50; Exodus 1–12). Although the Holy Spirit wasn't mentioned except in the verse when Pharaoh said Joseph had the Spirit of God in him, we can see the Holy Spirit's involvement in Joseph's life—by giving him dreams, helping him to interpret them, and strengthening him so he continued to serve God even though he was far away from home.

As the Israelites followed God into the desert, God called Moses up Mount Sinai and gave him the Ten Commandments as well as the instructions for building the tabernacle. God also filled and equipped people to do the work, "See, the Lord has called by name Bezalel…and He has filled him with the Spirit of God, in wisdom and understanding, in knowledge and all manner of workmanship, to design artistic works, to work in gold and silver and bronze; in cutting jewels for setting, in carving wood, and to work in all manner of artistic workmanship. And He has put in his heart the ability to teach, in him and Aholiab, the son of Ahisamach, of the tribe of Dan" (Exodus 35:30-34). God not only called people to do a job, He also gave them the ability and skills to do it.

Each one of us is born with God-given gifts and talents. Some people's talents are more obvious, and other people find it harder to find the place where they fit. When we develop the gifts and talents that we have received, we flow in our gifts and talents and the result is a fulfilled person who finds purpose in what they do. Before my husband finished high school, he knew he wanted to be an engineer. One time sitting around a table with a group of friends, he asked which of them knew what they wanted to do with their lives when they finished high school. Only two of the ten people knew. Sometimes people are impressed when they find out he is an engineer. Often people tell him he must be very clever. John always answers by saying that if he had to study languages or law or something else in college, he would have failed. Engineering is his gift, so it comes much more naturally to him than learning languages.

If a person studies or works in the area that they are gifted in, they will prosper. God is the greatest engineer in the universe. I have seen God give John an idea to fix a problem or give him wisdom to know what to do next with a project many times. If God designed the universe, don't you think He can help us solve the problems that we need to solve every day? My husband has learned that prayer and getting God involved in his job makes it easier. God knows the solution to every engineering problem. The Holy Spirit is also a Helper to engineers and those in the marketplace.

A friend once told me the important thing is not doing a job. God has a purpose with each of our lives and life is about finding that purpose and fulfilling it. A person's life's purpose can be to be an engineer, accountant, lawyer, teacher, stay-at-home mom, and so much more. If a person has a relationship with God, it should show in their work and relationships—by doing their work with integrity and by being faithful and honest.

Let us get back to the Israelites as they came out of Egypt and followed God into the desert. The journey was long and they started to complain. They remembered the fish and other food they ate in Egypt and complained about the manna they had to eat every day in the desert. Moses went to God and said, "Why are you treating me, your servant, so harshly? Have mercy on me! What did I do to deserve the burden of all these people?" (Numbers 11:11 NLT). Moses was carrying a burden that was too heavy for one person to carry. God told Moses to gather seventy elders as leaders of Israel and to bring them to the tabernacle to stand before the Lord, "And the Lord came down in the cloud and spoke to Moses. Then he gave the seventy elders the same Spirit that was upon Moses. And when the Spirit rested upon them, they prophesied" (Numbers 11:25 NLT).

Eldad and Medad were listed as elders; they stayed behind in the camp. The Spirit of the Lord rested upon them too and they started to prophesy. Prophesying was the manifestation seen when the Holy Spirit came upon these elders. Joshua told Moses to make them stop. Moses said he wished all the Lord's people were prophets and had His Spirit. What privileged days we live in. The Holy Spirit is not just limited to a few chosen vessels. Today the only requirement is believing in Jesus; so *all* of God's people can have His Holy Spirit, hear His voice, and tell others what He is saying.

After Moses died, Joshua stepped in as the next leader of Israel. God told Moses to lay hands on Joshua "a man in whom is the spirit" (Numbers 27:18). Moses laid hands on him and he was filled with the Spirit of Wisdom to lead Israel. Moses was one who was a friend of God, "Inside the Tent of Meeting, the Lord would speak to Moses face to face, as one speaks to a friend" (Exodus 33:11 NLT). When God assigned leaders to Israel, He filled them with His Spirit, but those leaders had to walk in relationship with God, be a friend of God, live a holy life, and obey God. We find that those who walked in a friendship relationship with God had a desire to know God. They trusted God with their lives, followed, and obeyed Him.

During the time of Gideon, the Israelites found themselves oppressed by the Midianites because "the children of Israel did evil in the sight of the Lord" (Judges 6:1). The Midianites raided their crops and the Israelites didn't have food. They cried out to God. God sent a prophet to the people; He also sent an angel to a man named Gideon. "Then the Spirit of the Lord clothed Gideon with power. He blew a ram's horn as a call to arms, and the men of the clan of Abiezer came to him" (Judges 6:34 NLT). The New King James reads, "the Spirit of the Lord came upon Gideon." The word "came" in this Scripture is the Hebrew word *labash* which means to put on clothes or be clothed.⁶ God needed a man who would be available to Him; and even though Gideon felt unfit for the job, God empowered him with His Holy Spirit to be the one to save the Israelites from that oppressive situation. You can read the rest of the story in Judges 6-8.

Time and again we read in the Old Testament that the Israelites did evil in the sight of the Lord and then God had to raise up a deliverer to help them. We see it again in Judges 13 when Samson was born. Samson had long hair which was a sign of a Nazirite, which means that his life was consecrated to God. We read about Samson that, "the Spirit of the Lord began to move upon him" (Judges 13:25) or "stir him" in the New Living Translation. When a lion attacked Samson, the Spirit of the Lord came upon him and Samson killed the lion (see Judges 14:6). Samson's strength came from God and he was used by God to deliver Israel from the Philistines (Judges 13-16).

King David was a remarkable man. David grew up as the youngest son of his father Jesse. God told the prophet Samuel to go and anoint the next king of Israel. He came into town to bring a sacrifice and invited Jesse and his sons to participate. He saw the first son, thinking *this is the one*. God told Samuel that He doesn't judge by a person's outward appearance, but He looks at the person's heart (1 Samuel 16:7). All seven sons came before Samuel, and he said that none of them were the one God has chosen.

Samuel asked if these were all of his children. Jesse said his youngest son was in the field, watching the sheep. They brought David to Samuel. "Samuel took the flask of olive oil he had brought and anointed David with the oil. And the Spirit of the Lord came powerfully upon David from that day on" (1 Samuel 16:13 NLT). The oil being poured on David was the physical act showing that he was set apart for a special job—to become king of Israel. We also see that God anointed David with the Holy Spirit to help him to be the king of Israel.

Saul was the king of Israel in the time of Samuel. He was disobedient to God. The Holy Spirit left him and tormenting spirits of fear and

---

6. Brown, Driver, Briggs, and Gesenius, "Hebrew Lexicon entry for *labash*," The KJV Old Testament Hebrew Lexicon, Accessed March 1, 2015, http://www.biblestudytools.com/lexicons/hebrew/kjv/labash.html.

depression troubled him (1 Samuel 16:14-15). David came to play the harp for Saul. Whenever David played the harp, the tormenting spirit left (1 Samuel 16:23). David knew how to release the presence of God when he played his harp. He went back and forth between helping his dad with the sheep and playing harp for Saul.

One day his dad sent him to take food to his brothers on the battlefield. David arrived at the battlefield as the Philistine giant, Goliath, was taunting Israel. David was disturbed by this giant speaking against God; he asked who would fight the giant. His question landed him before King Saul. Everyone was afraid to fight the giant, so David volunteered to do it. David knew God helped him when he was taking care of the sheep and he trusted that God will help him now too. As he approached Goliath, he revealed his faith in God, "You come to me with a sword, with a spear, and with a javelin. But I come to you in the name of the Lord of hosts, the God of the armies of Israel, whom you have defied" (1 Samuel 17:45). David defeated the giant with a slingshot and a stone. A dead giant made David famous. The same favor that Joseph walked in was upon David. Whatever King Saul asked him to do was a success. Saul became jealous of David and tried to kill him. David had to flee for his life (1 Samuel 18:5-11). He was on the run, hiding from Saul for several years.

Eventually the time came when David became king. David had weak moments as well as strong ones when he soared in his walk with God. He wasn't perfect. After he sinned with Bathsheba, he tried to cover it up by getting her husband Uriah killed in battle and marrying her. David always eventually turned back to God when he sinned, because his heart was tender toward God. At the end of David's life, he said, "The Spirit of the Lord speaks through me, his words are upon my tongue" (2 Samuel 23:2 NLT). And God said of David, "I have found David son of Jesse, a man after my own heart. He will do everything I want him to do" (Acts 13:22 NLT).

Daniel was another example of a true worshiper of God. He found himself in a very challenging situation when King Nebuchadnezzar's troops besieged Jerusalem during King Jehoiakim's reign. King Nebuchadnezzar ordered his chief of staff to bring strong, healthy, good-looking young men who had knowledge, understanding, and good judgment. Daniel and his friends were taken to the king's palace as captives. They were trained in the language and literature of Babylon. They were required to eat the king's food, which was not acceptable according to their Jewish laws. Daniel asked permission from the chief over them to allow them to eat vegetables and drink water for ten days and then examine their appearance. At the end of the trial period, they looked healthier than the other young men following the king's diet (Daniel 1:1-16). We read this about them: "God gave these four young men an unusual aptitude for understanding every aspect of literature and wisdom. And God gave Daniel the special ability to interpret the meanings of visions and dreams" (Daniel 1:17 NLT). The king was impressed with their wisdom and knowledge, and when he asked their advice it was far superior to the wisdom of the magicians (Daniel 1).

After King Nebuchadnezzar had a troubling dream, none of his magicians could relate it or interpret it. Daniel sought God and God showed him in a night vision what the dream was and what it meant. We see Daniel's boldness when he went before the king: "But there is a God in heaven who reveals secrets, and he has shown King Nebuchadnezzar what will happen in the future" (Daniel 2:28 NLT). Daniel described the king's dream about a huge statue of a man (Daniel 2). Daniel explained to the king that God made him the ruler of his empire, and after this conversation the king admitted that, "Truly, your God is the greatest of gods, the Lord over kings, a revealer of mysteries, for you have been able to reveal this secret" (Daniel 2:47 NLT). We need godly men and woman who can ask God to reveal wisdom and strategy to them too. Then the world will take notice and say, "Truly, your God is the greatest God."

Later King Nebuchadnezzar constructed a huge statue and sent for all the officials to come for its dedication. Every person was commanded to bow before the statue; any person who did not bow at the sounding of the horn would be thrown into a fire. Daniel's three friends, Shadrach, Meshach, and Abednego, refused to bow before the statue. The king gave them a second chance. They told the king that they would never disobey God and serve the Babylonian gods or the gold statue. The king was furious; they were thrown into the blazing furnace. The flames killed the soldiers who were ordered to throw them into the fire. A fourth man appeared in the fire with the three men and they were walking around in it unharmed. The king was amazed at this and called them out. The king was so touched by this event, he made a decree that no one was allowed to speak against the God of these men (Daniel 3). When we read the book of Daniel we can see that the uncompromising faith of Daniel and his three friends paid off. God showed up in the most impossible situations.

The king had another dream that his wise men couldn't interpret, and he called Daniel and said, "You are able, for the Spirit of the Holy God is in you" (Daniel 4:18). The dream was a serious warning and Daniel hesitated to interpret it for the king. He explained that the tree in the dream represented the king and his large kingdom. Daniel pleaded with the king, "King Nebuchadnezzar, please accept my advice. Stop sinning and do what is right. Break from your wicked past and be merciful to the poor. Perhaps then you will continue to prosper" (Daniel 4:27 NLT). King Nebuchadnezzar didn't listen to him and the dream came to its fulfillment: God struck the king and he became like an animal eating grass for seven years. At the end of that time, Nebuchadnezzar acknowledged and blessed God and declared that His kingdom is everlasting (Daniel 4). God can even turn the heart of an ungodly and proud king who does not believe in Him. He worked through men who did not compromise, even when their lives were at stake.

In Daniel, we witness four young Hebrew men taken out of their home country and placed into a king's court who doesn't serve their God. What do they do? They choose to stay true to the faith that they were taught in their homes. Their faith was severely challenged at times, but God rescued them from impossible situations. Under the rule of King Darius, Daniel didn't obey the king's decree regarding worship. The king said that if anyone worshiped any god other than the king they would be thrown into the lion's den. God rescued Daniel when he was thrown into the lion's den, because Daniel could not obey this decree. An angel came and shut the lions' mouths that they would not hurt him. The amazing thing is that this heathen king acknowledged this would happen, "Your God, whom you serve continually, He will deliver you" (Daniel 6:16). Then the king spent the night in fasting and praying for Daniel. When Daniel came out of the lion's den unharmed, the king made a new decree, "I make a decree that in every dominion of my kingdom men must tremble and fear before the God of Daniel. For He is the living God, and steadfast forever; His kingdom is the one which shall not be destroyed, and His dominion shall endure to the end. He delivers and rescues, and He works signs and wonders in heaven and on earth, who has delivered Daniel from the power of the lions" (Daniel 6:26-27). Daniel's strong faith and uncompromising stand turned a king's heart to believe in God.

And there are others in the Old Testament who responded to the working of the Holy Spirit. The prophet Azariah warned King Asa. When Asa heard the prophecy, he removed the idols from the land (2 Chronicles 15:1-8). Jahaziel spoke a prophetic word which encouraged the people to follow God with the result that God gave Jehoshaphat victory over his enemies (2 Chronicles 20:13-18). God gave King Solomon great wisdom and understanding (1 Kings 4:29-34). Ezekiel prophesied about a time where God would put His Spirit in His people and they would obey Him. "And I will put my Spirit in you so that you will follow my decrees and be careful to obey my regulations" (Ezekiel 36:27 NLT). The prophet Micah said he was filled with power from the Holy Spirit (Micah 3:8).

When the Holy Spirit came upon a person, something supernatural happened and the result was change. God raised up deliverers again and again to free the Israelites from captivity because of their own sins. God gave them prophet after prophet to speak the truth to them. Most of the time they didn't want to listen. God in His mercy moved upon and through people again and again, to bring deliverance and to bring the people back to His ways.

We find a powerful message from God to Zerubbabel in Zechariah 4:6: "'Not by might nor by power, but by My Spirit,' says the Lord of hosts." We can take heed of that message too—in our strength and power we will not get the job done. We need God's Holy Spirit for wisdom, strength, and power. He is available to us, so why wouldn't we receive Him and walk with Him to be more fruitful in our lives?

Discussion Questions: Where Is the Holy Spirit in the Old Testament?

1. Which of the Old Testament accounts made the biggest impression on you? Why?

   _____
   _____
   _____
   _____
   _____

2. What can you learn from Joseph's life (Genesis 37, 39-45) that can be helpful in your own life?

   _____
   _____
   _____
   _____
   _____

3. Share some wisdom from Daniel's life that you can use in your own life.

   _____
   _____
   _____
   _____
   _____

4. What was the importance of the Holy Spirit in the Old Testament?

_____
_____
_____
_____
_____
_____

5. Choose one of the following Scriptures to ponder: Zechariah 4:6; 2 Chronicles 20:6; Exodus 31:3-5; or Numbers 11:29. You can look at cross-references or simply read the Scripture in context. Let the Holy Spirit lead you.

Chapter 3: Did Jesus Have the Holy Spirit?

"Jesus traveled all through Galilee teaching in the Jewish synagogues, everywhere preaching the Good News of the Kingdom of Heaven. And he healed every kind of sickness and disease. The report of his miracles spread far beyond the borders of Galilee so that sick folk were soon coming to be healed from as far away as Syria. And whatever their illness and pain, or if they were possessed by demons, or were insane, or paralyzed—he healed them all" (Matthew 4:23 TLB).

The life of Jesus was extraordinary from the beginning. His mother, Mary, was a virgin (Isaiah 7:14; Matthew 1:22-23). When the angel appeared to Mary to tell her she will become pregnant with the baby Jesus, he said, "The Holy Spirit will come upon you, and the power of the Most High will overshadow you [like a shining cloud]" (Luke 1:35 AMP). What a life-changing encounter this was for Mary; she met an angel and then became pregnant with Jesus, Son of the living God. The Holy Spirit brings forth the will of God on earth. Mary gave her permission and said, "I am the Lord's servant. May everything you have said about me come true" (Luke 1:38 NLT). The Holy Spirit is looking for willing vessels to bring forth God's will on earth—whether it is to deliver a word of encouragement, to pray for someone, or help one in need. We are the hands and feet of Jesus on earth. God knew each one of us before we were born; David said, "You watched me as I was being formed in utter seclusion, as I was woven together in the dark of the womb" (Psalm 139:15 NLT).

When Joseph, Mary's fiancé, heard that she was pregnant he secretly wanted to break the engagement. An angel appeared to him in a dream and confirmed to him that Mary's baby was from God and conceived by the Holy Spirit. Further he was told that they should call the baby Jesus and that He would save people from their sins (Matthew 1:20-22). During this time Caesar Augustus released a decree that everyone should be registered in a census in their home town. Joseph traveled with a very pregnant Mary to Bethlehem. They arrived in Bethlehem to find the town full and no place to stay. The only place they found was a stable where the heavenly King was born that night. Angels appeared to shepherds and told them about the Savior's birth. They went to Bethlehem to find the newborn King. Interestingly God told the least important people, shepherds in a field, that His Son was born.

When Jesus was eight days old, Joseph and Mary took Him to the temple to bring the required sacrifice. A priest named Simeon lived in Jerusalem at this time. The Bible tells us that the Holy Spirit was upon Simeon and had revealed to him that he would not die before he saw the Messiah (Luke 2:25-32). That day the Holy Spirit compelled Simeon to go to the temple at the same time Jesus was being dedicated. I experienced something similar to this. At the time I didn't go to our local house of prayer on Mondays. That day I just felt like I needed to go. Later in the day I knew it was the Holy Spirit who had compelled me to go. God had a divine appointment for me there that day. Someone from out of town stopped by, and because I was there, I was able to talk and pray with them.

Simeon and Anna had divine appointments too. Simeon took Jesus in his arms and prophesied over Him: "He is a light to reveal God to the nations" (Luke 2:32 NLT). Simeon blessed Jesus and prophetically declared His destiny. Anna was a widow who regularly went to the temple to fast and pray. When she saw Joseph, Mary, and Jesus, she began praising God for the child. She went out and told everyone that the promised king was born (Luke 2:36-38). The Holy Spirit revealed to Simeon and Anna that Jesus was the long-awaited Messiah. The wise men saw the star and followed it to find the newborn King of the Jews (Matthew 2:2). God revealed that the baby Jesus was the Messiah to only a few people. God did not reveal this information to the high priest or the other priests. He found hungry hearts in Simeon and Anna. He spoke to those who were seeking Him, "But without faith it is impossible to please Him, for he who comes to God must believe that He is, and that He is a rewarder of those who diligently seek Him" (Hebrews 11:6).

My foundation as a Christian was formed at a church that placed great value in spending personal time with God daily, diligently pursuing Him. Learning about the value of intimacy with God was very beneficial to my spiritual growth. Though there were days I missed, this habit has kept me on track. My focus on being diligent in my relationship with God has been good for me. There were times when I received a great deal from Him and other times when He didn't speak very much at all, and it didn't feel like anything was happening. Focusing on being diligent kept me going at these times. My habit taught me to not be focused on results. I understood that there would always be times when I heard from God a lot and other more quiet seasons. I have grown a great deal in my relationship in walking with God, Jesus, and the Holy Spirit by focusing on being diligent in seeking Him.

The grace of God was upon Jesus as a child. "And the Child grew and became strong in spirit, filled with wisdom; and the grace of God was upon Him" (Luke 2:40). When Jesus was twelve years old, He went to Jerusalem with His parents to celebrate the Passover Feast. When Mary and Joseph left Jerusalem on their journey home, they couldn't find Jesus. They turned back and found Him in the temple sitting amongst the religious teachers discussing questions with them. The group was amazed by His understanding. The Holy Spirit was working in Jesus' life, giving Him understanding beyond His years. As Jesus grew physically, He also grew in wisdom, maturity, and favor with God and men (Luke 2:52).

Later the Holy Spirit told John the Baptist that the One on whom he saw the Holy Spirit descend and rest was the Messiah. John witnessed the Holy Spirit descending like a dove upon Jesus, "and He remained upon Him" (John 1:32). When God released Jesus into ministry, He was clothed in the Holy Spirit—the anointing or presence of God to do miracles and to walk in the power of God. The Holy Spirit led Jesus into the desert where He fasted for forty days. During this time when He was very hungry, the Devil tempted Him. Jesus responded to every temptation with Scripture. The Scriptures that Jesus learned during His childhood were in Him and He could use them (Matthew 4:1-10). After the last temptation, Jesus said, "Away with you, Satan! For it is written, *'You shall worship the Lord your God, and Him only you shall serve'*" (Matthew 4:10). Satan left and God sent angels to minister to Jesus.

Jesus fulfilled the prophecy of the prophet Isaiah, "Behold! My Servant whom I have chosen, My Beloved in whom My soul is well pleased! I will put My Spirit upon Him, and He will declare justice to the Gentiles… A bruised reed He will not break" (Matthew 12:18, 20; see also Isaiah 42:1-4). The first part was fulfilled at Jesus' baptism (Matthew 3:16). The Holy Spirit came upon Jesus, clothing Him with power to do miracles. Many in Israel expected a Messiah who would rescue them from Roman oppression. Jesus came to set spiritual captives free: "For he has rescued us from the kingdom of darkness and transferred us into the Kingdom of his dear Son, who purchased our freedom and forgave our sins" (Colossians 1:13-14 NLT). Jesus needed the power of the Holy Spirit to heal people, to set captives free, and raise the dead (Luke 4:18).

The Gospels say Jesus had compassion for the people when He saw the crowds (Mark 1:41; 6:34; 8:2). Even though Jesus was the Son of God, He never looked down upon anyone. He never thought that any person was not worth helping. The Living Bible reads, "He does not crush the weak, or quench the smallest hope" (Matthew 12:20). This is so comforting. We have all felt discouraged at times. Jesus came to give hope to the hopeless, "his name will be the hope of all the world" (Matthew 12:21 NLT). Jesus lived the fruit of the Holy Spirit (Galatians 5:22-23). He healed the sick, blind, deaf, and lame, and showed love and compassion to people. The Pharisees were upset that Jesus didn't separate Himself from sinners, but ate with them and spent time with sinners instead (Matthew 9:11). Jesus didn't spend much time arguing with those bound by religious traditions. He spoke truth. They could have received it, but chose to avoid His words and present trick questions to gather evidence to convict Him instead.

Jesus modeled a life of total surrender to God, obeying His Father, and living in the power of the Holy Spirit. From His youth, He showed unusual understanding of the Scriptures when He asked the religious teachers questions and gave them surprising answers to their questions to Him (Luke 2:47). After His baptism when the Holy Spirit came upon Him, the people were astonished by the authority Jesus had. Jesus' teaching was not like the teaching of the scribes; He taught with true authority (Matthew 7:28-29). John the Baptist said of Jesus that He is sent by God, He speaks God's words, He has the Spirit without limitation, and God gave Him authority over everything (John 3:34-35). He told stories in the form of parables to the people to explain truth. Jesus had authority over sickness, leprosy, blindness, deafness, and He even raised people from the dead. He also had authority over nature and rebuked the storm to be silent (Mark 4:39). We receive the indwelling Holy Spirit when we accept Jesus, but we also need the empowering work of the Holy Spirit to do what He has called us to do. We can ask Him to empower us.

Jesus did not walk in this authority, making other people feel inferior or less important. He lived in dependence upon God. He listened to His Father and followed and obeyed His Father's voice (John 5:19). John 5:30 is a key verse to how Jesus walked on earth:

> "I am able to do nothing from Myself [independently, of My own accord—but only as I am taught by God and as I get His orders]. Even as I hear, I judge [I decide as I am bidden to decide. As the voice comes to Me, so I give a decision], and My judgment is right (just, righteous), because I do not seek or consult My own will [I have no desire to do what is pleasing to myself, My own aim, My own purpose] but only the will and pleasure of the Father Who sent Me" (John 5:30 AMP).

There are many key truths in this verse. Jesus didn't operate independently from His Father. He heard His Father's voice and obeyed Him. Jesus had to discern who was speaking to Him—was it God, was it Himself, was it the Devil, or another person's opinion? The reason Jesus made the right choice was because He laid down His own will and His own desires. He lived to do the will of His Father. When we hear the Holy Spirit, we need to set aside our own desires too. Otherwise our hearing can be in error. That was the reason God exalted Jesus and gave

Him the name above every other name. Jesus laid down His life and desires even unto death and God exalted Him to the highest position, sitting at the right hand of the Father. God has exalted the name of Jesus above every other name (Philippians 2:5-11).

When Jesus multiplied the five loaves and two fish, He looked up to heaven and thanked God for the food. The disciples distributed it and it was enough to feed 5,000 people (Matthew 14:19)! This is just one example of Jesus' communication with His Father—and its results. Jesus often spent time by Himself in the night praying (Matthew 14:23; Mark 6:46). If Jesus needed to spend time with God and needed to pray, how much more do we need to do the same. We have the ability to invite the Creator of the universe into our day. We were given the authority by Jesus to open and close doors in the spirit (Matthew 18:18). Through prayer, we can affect the world around us according to the will of God. The Devil seeks to discourage us from praying. If he can keep us from praying, we won't affect what happens around us. This is just one more reason why we need to know the voice of God above all others. May He direct us through His Holy Spirit to pray and walk in the way He has chosen.

Jesus said that many will prophesy and do miracles in His name and at the judgment day, He will say to some of these, "I never knew you" (Matthew 7:23). The word "knew" in the Greek is *ginosko* which means "to learn to know, to come to know"; it has a reference to intimacy between husband and wife. This refers to a deeper knowing.[7] Jesus spent time with His Father. He walked on earth in relationship with His Father. Our relationship with God needs to be the same as His, a dependence upon God, living a life of prayer and being connected to the Holy Spirit to hear and feel what is on our Father's heart for our lives. This relationship will propel us into the destiny God has planned for our lives.

Jesus said He cast demons out by the power of the Holy Spirit (Matthew 12:28). It was a sign that the kingdom of God was breaking in amongst them. Jesus taught the disciples to pray "On earth as it is in heaven" (Matthew 6:10). When a person receives healing or is set free, the kingdom of God

---
7. Gerhard Kittel and Gerhard Friedrich, *Theological Dictionary of the New Testament*, s.v. "Ginosko," accessed March 1, 2015, http://www.biblestudytools.com/lexicons/greek/kjv/ginosko.html.

breaks in. When people make the right choices, the kingdom of God is established. We know there is no sickness, demonic oppression, bitterness, hatred, jealousy, etc. in heaven (Galatians 5:19-21).

When I see a need and help—whether it is to pray for the sick, feed the hungry, encourage the weak, strengthen those who are discouraged, or share the good news of Jesus—I am bringing God's kingdom to earth. Even to listen to someone share their problems can be helpful. People process challenging situations by talking about them and may receive insight as they talk it through. Just to respond with, *"How did that make you feel?"* or *"I can see that was a very challenging situation for you"* can be the best thing for someone trying to find their way. After we have listened, we can ask the person if we can pray with them, asking that God will comfort, bring breakthrough, or the help that is needed.

Jesus read the prophecy from Isaiah 61 in the local synagogue after His baptism and forty days in the desert. He said, "The Spirit of the Lord is upon Me, because He has anointed Me to preach the gospel to the poor. He has sent Me to heal the brokenhearted, to proclaim liberty to the captives, and recovery of sight to the blind, to set at liberty those who are oppressed" (Luke 4:18). Jesus cast devils out of people by the power of the Holy Spirit (Matthew 12:28). He traveled through Galilee teaching in the synagogues, healing people from every kind of sickness and disease (Matthew 4:23).

When Lazarus died, Jesus didn't immediately go to his house. By the time He arrived Lazarus had been dead four days. We read that He purposefully waited. He told His disciples that Lazarus was dead, and that this was happening that they would come to really believe in Him. When they finally arrived, they found Mary and Martha weeping over their brother's death. Jesus lifted up His eyes and thanked God that He heard Him, "Then Jesus shouted, 'Lazarus, come out!'" (John 11:43 NLT). What an amazing miracle! Jesus knew God wanted Him to wait before He went to Lazarus' house. In the natural, it didn't make sense—Jesus was good friends with Lazarus and his sisters. Why wouldn't He go to them as soon as He could? Jesus knew God's voice well enough that He could wait and obey even though circumstances tried to point Him in a different direction, urging Him to do things differently. But He listened to God with the result that God was glorified and His disciples were bolstered in their faith.

Later Jesus healed a paralyzed man and told him his sins were forgiven. The religious leaders were upset. They said this was blasphemy, that only God can forgive sins. Jesus immediately knew what they were thinking in His spirit (Mark 2:8). How was that possible? Jesus walked on earth and showed us how to live in relationship with God. He spent time in prayer at night and heard the Holy Spirit speak or reveal what He should do. The Holy Spirit revealed even people's thoughts to Jesus as He was going around preaching, teaching, and healing the sick.

Philip was one of the men Jesus called to be a disciple. Philip told Nathaniel about Jesus. When Nathaniel approached Jesus, Jesus said; "Behold, an Israelite indeed, in whom is no deceit!" (John 1:47). Nathaniel asked Jesus how He knew him. Jesus told him he saw him as he sat under the fig tree. Jesus wasn't there when Philip met Nathaniel under the tree. Jesus saw Nathaniel in the spirit and the Holy Spirit revealed to Him that Nathaniel was a godly Israelite. This may have worked like this: Jesus saw a picture of Nathaniel sitting under the fig tree in His mind and at the same time knew in the Spirit of God that he was a godly Israelite.

When Jesus asked the disciples to prepare the Passover Feast, He gave them very specific instructions. He told them to go into the city and find a man carrying a water pitcher. They should follow him to the house he entered and ask the owner, "The Teacher asks: 'Where is the guest room where I can eat the Passover meal with my disciples?'" (Mark 14:14 NLT). This was revelation from the Holy Spirit too. Jesus didn't say *God told me*, He just acted naturally and obeyed the instructions His Father gave Him through the Holy Spirit. The Holy Spirit showed Jesus what to do in every situation.

The Holy Spirit was also present at the crucifixion: "Under the old system, the blood of goats and bulls and the ashes of a young cow could cleanse people's bodies from ceremonial impurity. Just think how much more the blood of Christ will purify our consciences from sinful deeds so that we can worship the living God. For by the power of the eternal Spirit, Christ offered himself to God as a perfect sacrifice for our sins"

(Hebrews 9:14 NLT). Jesus needed the Holy Spirit to endure the cross. In my everyday life, I ask God for grace to do the things He wants me to do. How much more should we ask for grace in a difficult situation.

It was the power of the Holy Spirit that raised Jesus from the dead. "The Spirit of God, who raised Jesus from the dead, lives in you. And just as God raised Christ Jesus from the dead, he will give life to your mortal bodies by this same Spirit living within you" (Romans 8:11 NLT). The Holy Spirit who raised Jesus from the dead is the One by whose power we will receive our resurrected bodies (1 Corinthians 15:51-52). After His resurrection, Jesus appeared to the disciples, "until the day he was taken up to heaven after giving his chosen apostles further instructions through the Holy Spirit" (Acts 1:2 NLT). He talked to them about the kingdom of God and He told them to wait in Jerusalem until God gave them the promised Holy Spirit, "John baptized with water, but in just a few days you will be baptized with the Holy Spirit" (Acts 1:5 NLT).

Jesus came to earth to die and pay for our sins. He also showed us how to live a natural supernatural life. He regularly spent time with His Father, usually in the evenings (Matthew 14:23; Mark 6:46). He didn't operate in His own strength (John 14:10; 5:30). He listened to the voice of His Father and obeyed what His Father told Him to do. He operated in the power of the Holy Spirit. Before Jesus left He told the disciples, "And I will pray the Father, and He will give you another Helper, that He may abide with you forever—the Spirit of truth, whom the world cannot receive, because it neither sees Him nor knows Him; but you know Him, for He dwells with you and will be in you" (John 14:16-17). This is Jesus' desire—when we receive Him as the Lord of our lives, we will not live as orphans but will know He has given us a Helper.

I ask the Holy Spirit to help me daily, to reveal truth from the Bible, to lead and guide me in my life. I have learned to hear His voice in my everyday life and problems. I have seen how He comes and helps me. Surprising things happen when I ask Him to lead me and show me what is on His agenda for my life. I have my schedule, but pray about it as I am starting a new year or when situations change. My life is more productive and I feel at peace when I walk in step with what Jesus wants me to do as much as I can.

Discovering the Holy Spirit

Follow the example of Jesus. He made provision for us to live a life of peace and to overcome—no matter what we face. It doesn't always happen in an instant, but Jesus knows the way and He has given us the Holy Spirit to help us. I recently heard the testimony of a pastor who had cancer. God often gave him words for others. During that challenging time, he didn't hear the voice of God. God spoke to him and encouraged him through others. He asked many people to pray for him and used the Word against the sickness. He overcame.

In our walk with God, we go through different seasons. We go through times when God feels very near, and we go through challenges and even times of testing when it feels like God is far away. Even though God is still as close as our next breath, our awareness of Him just changes. God doesn't always speak everything to us directly; sometimes we have to receive His word through others. This process keeps us humble and seeking Him. We do not know exactly what He is going to do or how. This is why we need our brothers and sisters in Christ.

A lady, who teaches others to hear God's voice, shared how she did not experience God's presence for a year. She was used to experiencing His presence. The Holy Spirit told her God was teaching her to walk by faith and not by what she feels. She said it was hard for her when others around her would share how they felt God's presence and she felt nothing. This is a very important lesson to learn, because it often happens in our worst crises that we don't hear from God or don't receive the insight we need. We must hold on to the facts: He is with us. He hears our prayers. He knows what He is doing even when things don't make sense to us. In the natural, it didn't make sense for Jesus to wait three days before going to resurrect Lazarus from the dead. Yet, that was God's time and Jesus obeyed. When we get to the place in our faith that we can bless God and keep our faith and trust in Him no matter what happens, we are maturing as Christians. "Bless the Lord, O my soul; and all that is within me, bless His holy name!" (Psalm 103:1). Even Jesus experienced this in the garden of Gethsemane when He sweat blood, and on the cross when He said, "My God, My God, why have You *forsaken* Me?"(Mark 15:34).

Hermie Reynolds

Discussion Questions: Did Jesus Have the Holy Spirit?

1. Jesus went through a time of learning. What is noticeable to you about His life as a child and growing up?

_____
_____
_____
_____

2. Discuss what happened when Jesus was baptized (Matthew 3:13-17; John 1:31-33). John the Baptist said, "For he is sent by God. He speaks God's words, for God gives him the Spirit without limit" (John 3:34 NLT).

_____
_____
_____
_____

3. Jesus acted normally while having the Holy Spirit without limit. Discuss this Scripture in John 3:34. What does it look like to have the Spirit without limit?

_____
_____
_____
_____

Discovering the Holy Spirit

4. Isaiah prophesied of Jesus that the Spirit will be upon Him and, "A bruised reed He will not break, and a dimly burning wick He will not quench; He will bring forth justice in truth" (Isaiah 42:3 AMP). This is how the Holy Spirit responds to us too. Discuss: Do you see Him this way?

_____

_____

_____

5. The Holy Spirit is the One who helps us when we go through difficult times. "This is what I have asked of God for you: that you will be encouraged and knit together by strong ties of love, and that you will have the rich experience of knowing Christ with real certainty and clear understanding" (Colossians 2:2 TLB). Discuss how He has helped you through trouble and trials.

_____

_____

_____

_____

6. Choose a phrase or Scripture from Philippians 2:1-11 and ask the Holy Spirit to speak to you. Write down what He says.

_____

_____

_____

_____

_____

Chapter 4: How Does the Holy Spirit Work in Me?

> "Nevertheless I tell you the truth. It is to your advantage that I go away; for if I do not go away, the Helper will not come to you; but if I depart, I will send Him to you. And when He has come, He will convict the world of sin, and of righteousness, and of judgment" (John 16:7-8).

We read accounts in the Bible in which God radically intervened in a person's life. Jonah ended up in the belly of a whale because he didn't want to deliver God's message to the people of Nineveh. Jacob saw a ladder going up and down and wrestled with God (Genesis 28:12). Moses met God at a burning bush (Exodus 3:2). Joshua saw the sun stand still, and God gave the Israelites victory over the Amorites (Joshua 10:13). God sent supernatural fire from heaven to ignite the altar when Elijah prayed (1 Kings 18:38). An angel visited Mary (Luke 1:30), and Paul was knocked down, blinded by a bright light while Jesus spoke to him (Acts 9:3-6). God usually speaks through the soft voice of the Holy Spirit. On occasion God breaks through in a supernatural way to get a person's attention when that person will not hear what God has to say in His soft inner voice.

During the reign of King Belshazzar a hand appeared and wrote on the wall. The king was greatly troubled by this and called in his wise men, but they couldn't interpret it. The message that Daniel gave to the king revealed God's sovereignty over everything, "Listen, O king! The High God gave your father Nebuchadnezzar a great kingdom and a glorious reputation. Because God made him so famous, people from everywhere, whatever their race, color, and creed, were totally intimidated by him. He killed or spared people on whim. He promoted or humiliated people capriciously. He developed a big head and a hard spirit. Then God knocked him off his high horse and stripped him of his fame" (Daniel 5:18-20 MSG). God warned King Nebuchadnezzar in a dream, but he didn't listen and humble himself. The result was that God humbled him and he ate grass for seven years. When he came to his senses and came out of this experience, he said:

> "At the end of the seven years, I, Nebuchadnezzar, looked to heaven. I was given my mind back and I blessed the High God, thanking and glorifying God, who lives forever. His sovereign rule lasts and lasts, his kingdom never declines and falls. Life on this earth doesn't add up to much, but God's heavenly army keeps everything going. No one can interrupt his work, no one can call his rule into question. At the same time that I was given back my mind, I was also given back my majesty and splendor, making my kingdom shine. All the leaders and important people came looking for me. I was reestablished as king in my kingdom and became greater than ever. And that's why I'm singing—I, Nebuchadnezzar—singing and praising the King of Heaven: Everything he does is right, and he does it the right way. He knows how to turn a proud person into a humble man or woman" (Daniel 4:34-36 MSG).

It took a lot for God to break through to Nebuchadnezzar. God warned him through a dream about his pride. Daniel interpreted the dream and told him what would happen. Nebuchadnezzar didn't listen, but after seven years of living like an animal, he acknowledged God as sovereign. Nebuchadnezzar's son walked the same path of pride and a hardened heart. God spoke to King Belshazzar through the handwriting on the wall. Daniel came and interpreted it to him. God said his time had run out. That same night the king died and the empire was divided between the Medes and the Persians (Daniel 4 and 5).

God gave Adam and Eve a free will to make choices (Genesis 3:1-7). He gave them each a conscience, an inner awareness of right and wrong. Our conscience operates in connection with our will. In Romans 9:1,

Paul says, "With Christ as my witness, I speak with utter truthfulness. My conscience and the Holy Spirit confirm it" (Romans 9:1 NLT). We have the choice to develop a tender conscience that keeps us from sinning or we can harden our hearts. On the one hand we see a person can lay down their own will and follow God's plan for their lives, or a person's God-given conscience can harden to such a degree that the person can choose to hate and do evil deeds. We are not born with a hard heart, but we can develop a hard heart through life. What people are taught can cause them to have a hard heart and conscience. Hardship can cause a person to harden their hearts too. The wealth and luxuries of this world can cause a person to think, *I've got it made. My life and my future are in my own hands. I can do whatever I want*. That is false security and there comes a day when the person realizes that no amount of wealth or possessions will fill the void in their heart.

When you keep your heart tender, it will help you to be more aware of how God's Spirit is working in and around you, and you will become more sensitive to His voice. In the book of Acts we read about Paul and Silas that "the Holy Spirit had prevented them from preaching the word in the province of Asia at that time" (Acts 16:6 NLT). In verse 7 we read, "Then coming to the borders of Mysia, they headed north for the province of Bithynia, but again the Spirit of Jesus did not allow them to go there" (Acts 16:7 NLT). The Holy Spirit prevented them through an inward witness; they knew they were not supposed to go there. That night Paul had a vision about a man from Macedonia asking them to come and help them. Paul and Silas interpreted this vision as God calling them to Macedonia. The apostles received direction from the Holy Spirit to show them where to go and preach. Even though God was in charge of their travels, it didn't mean they didn't go through hardship or have challenges. Even so, God was with them through it all.

The Holy Spirit Convicts People of Sin

> "And when he (Holy Spirit) has come he will convince the world of its sin, and of the availability of God's goodness and of deliverance from judgment. The world's sin is unbelief in me" (John 16:8-9 TLB).

Discovering the Holy Spirit

The Holy Spirit works in the hearts of people to convict them of sin and bring them to the place where they realize that they need a Savior and they need to turn their lives and hearts to Jesus. God doesn't force anyone to receive Jesus. He has made salvation available to everyone. God will ask every person: *What did you do with my Son, Jesus?* When the Holy Spirit has brought us to the point that we come to believe in Jesus, confess that we are a sinner, and receive Him as our Savior, He comes and lives inside of us. He continues this journey with us and works in us through a process of sanctification, cleaning up our lives so that we can be more like Jesus (2 Thessalonians 2:13).

> "There is an ongoing warfare, a struggle between our natural desires, and His spiritual desire for us. Thus, there are two contrary wills at war with each other—*I will* and *Thy will*. When we choose *Thy will* (His purpose for us), which is contrary to and crosses *I will* (our wants), our cross is formed. As I die to my own will, and submit to and come into alignment with His will for me, I am indeed taking up my cross, thereby becoming *'one'* with Him in intention and purpose."[8]

It is often crisis situations or challenges that draw us to search for God. Challenges in my life turned me to seeking God. I grew up in church, but didn't have a personal relationship with God. God didn't wait; the Holy Spirit drew me to the Christian bookstore where I found the right book that He used to reveal to me that I needed Jesus. God connected me with the right people and I surrendered my life to Jesus. Although surrendering my life to Jesus brought me great joy, not everything in my soul immediately changed. The emotional wounds and hurts were still there, hidden, below the surface.

I met my husband a year into this journey, and a year after that we got married. The Holy Spirit worked in both our lives. We attended a local church of a mainline denomination in South Africa. A visiting pastor from the United States led our church in prayer meetings for a week every morning from five to six in the morning; about 500 people attended. This pastor compiled a booklet with prayers for personal

---
8. Wade E. Taylor, *Waterspouts of Glory, Volume One,* (Greensboro, NC: Wade Taylor Publications, 1995), 101.

repentance and repentance about relationships with family, friends, and coworkers. I can remember how life changing that week was for us. Who could have imagined the joy we would receive by going to church at 5 a.m. and spending an hour repenting and praying. We felt revived and full of renewed zeal for God. The purpose of the week was to launch people into a habit of spending time with God every morning. It was a blessed beginning to my many mornings with Jesus.

It is not easy to admit that we have done wrong and to go to someone and ask forgiveness for sin. Our pride gets injured when we find ourselves in a position where we have to say we're sorry. I think my marriage is the place where I found myself most often in this situation. I think it is harder for men to admit when they are wrong. But God tells us to humble ourselves. If we humble ourselves and repent when we need to, God doesn't have to humble us and bring us to repentance. Repentance means to turn away from sin and wrongdoing.

One day one of our children said, "Mommies cry, but daddies don't cry." It's true that I cry easily. I cry when I am happy and I cry when I am sad. My kids have seen their mom cry a lot. That day though, I realized this was my son's perception—men don't cry. I had to purposely try and help the boys not to shut down their emotions and live out the "men don't cry" image. The fact is this: crying is not what is important, but shutting down one's emotions can do a lot of harm. I know this because that is what I did growing up. I shut out the rejection that I experienced from the lack of my dad's involvement in my life.

When our children were in elementary school, my husband and I attended a conference about the Father-heart of God. He came back from that conference with a tender heart. When we came home, he sat down with our children and apologized that he had misrepresented God's love and character. He also gave them permission to tell us when we were not treating them the right way. There have been a few times when they came and talked to us about times when we hurt their feelings. God has used that time to bring restoration in our family.

Repentance is freeing. It cleanses the slate between us and God. The Holy Spirit will bring conviction when we need it. Condemnation comes from the enemy and keeps us feeling bad, without anything changing for the better. When we ask for forgiveness, it is like pressing delete on a computer. We ask for forgiveness and God presses delete. The enemy remembers what we did and tries to condemn us. If we have wronged another person, the Holy Spirit might want us to go and make it right with the person. Many years ago I read Psalm 32:8-9: "I will instruct you (says the Lord) and guide you along the best pathway for your life; I will advise you and watch your progress. Don't be like a senseless horse or a mule that has to have a bit in its mouth to keep it in line" (TLB). Back then I told God that I would rather learn from other people's mistakes and the Bible than continually make my own mistakes and learn by them. The Holy Spirit has been faithful. He teaches me through books, the lives of others, messages that I have heard, and living life. It is not that I never make mistakes, but I don't just learn the hard way.

The Holy Spirit Transforms Our Lives

> "But whenever someone turns to the Lord, the veil is taken away...So all of us who have had that veil removed can see and reflect the glory of the Lord. And the Lord—who is the Spirit—makes us more and more like him as we are changed into his glorious image" (2 Corinthians 3:16, 18 NLT).

The Amplified Bible reads "behold [in the Word of God] as in a mirror the glory of the Lord." The most important tool the Holy Spirit uses to bring transformation in our lives is the Bible. Early in my walk with Jesus, I often read the Amplified Bible. As we read the Bible, we see areas in which our lives do not reflect Jesus. The Holy Spirit reveals the places we should change. The Holy Spirit used the verse in Matthew 7:1-2 to bring change in my life, "Do not judge and criticize and condemn others, so that you may not be judged and criticized and condemned yourselves" (AMP).

The week I read that verse, He showed me how judgmental I was at times. He also showed me how people judge others through the lens of their own experience. Then He showed me God's perspective—how God would answer someone's prayer and supply a blessing that I thought wasn't a necessity. God looks at the hearts. He can give one person a blessing and for the next person say, *If I give you this desire now, it will not be good for you.* It was a good lesson to learn because we so easily compare ourselves to other people. We tend to look at material possessions and call someone who has many things blessed.

Friends visited us one weekend and asked us how our kids were doing. My friend asked me what words they have received over their lives. After I shared with her, she said, "one is called to a greater walk of faith, trusting God for provision; and the other one has favor that opens doors for him in the area of work." It was helpful for me to hear this, because I knew how challenging it was at times for my one son who was called to a greater walk of faith. We tend to come up with formulas or recipes; we reason that if this is how it worked for one person, it should work the same way for others. Then we find out that God doesn't do it that way. He has a special plan for each person. We can learn from one another's experiences, but He doesn't have one blueprint. He does not work through a cookie-cutter process.

I have attended many prayer training seminars and read several books that have helped me grow. One of the most helpful spiritual laws I have learned is about sowing and reaping. When we sow negative seeds of judgment or offense, we will reap them again later in a similar situation (Galatians 6:7). For example, the commandment to honor our parents is found in both the Old and New Testaments (Exodus 20:12; Matthew 15:4; Ephesians 6:2). This commandment has the promise of a long life connected to it. When everything goes well, this is not a problem, but when there are problems in the family or abuse, this can be challenging. If there is abuse, it is easy to understand that the parent did something wrong, and the person needs to forgive them and let it go. For me it was a bit harder to recognize, because my dad was working hard and just wasn't home much. How could I be angry with him for that? Later I learned that a lack of attention and affection can also have a negative effect on a child.

One day as I was reading a book about the Christian family, the Holy Spirit revealed the judgments I carried in my heart against my dad. My husband was working from home at the time. Our garage had been remodeled into office space. The Holy Spirit showed me how my husband worked during the day, ate dinner with us, and then continued to work many evenings just like my dad had. As I read about a father's role in the family, I repented of my judgments against my own dad. He wasn't emotionally there for me. It felt like he had never made time for me, didn't protect me, and just wasn't there for me like he should have been. My husband was away for business that day. When he came home he found a transformed wife. We were in the midst of one of those times when it felt like there was an invisible wall between us that made communication impossible. When he came home that evening he found a very different wife than the one he had left that morning.

When I repented of my judgments against my dad, it tore down the wall between my husband and me. When we talked to each other afterward, we found that he thought I was mad at him about something that was not even a problem. The enemy had used the judgments I was holding to build a stronghold in my husband based on a lie. What all my nagging and complaining couldn't change, repenting of my judgments against my dad accomplished. Men often have judgments about their mothers. A mother tells her children to do the right thing so often that it is easy for a boy to judge his mom in that area. This will carry over into his relationships with women, especially his wife. The husband will feel that his wife is critical about everything he does.

I taught my children from an early age about judgments. When our oldest son was in first grade the teacher had to leave the class for a short while. She left one of the girls in charge who had to report back to her about who talked while she was gone. When the teacher came back the girl reported that all the boys and one girl talked. The teacher lined up the offenders and said she was taking them to the principal. They didn't walk far when all the little ones started to cry. The next morning my son didn't want to go to school. I had a hard time getting him dressed. Every morning it was the same story—he didn't want to go to school. Eventually we decided to put the kids in a private school. Everything was fine for a while until one day our son got into trouble again. The next day we had the same problem—he refused to go to school. I went to talk to the teacher, but it did not seem that the incident at school was such a big deal that it should cause such a response from my son. I pressed into prayer, "God, what is going on?"

A few days later the Holy Spirit revealed to me my son's judgment against the first teacher and how he was reaping it in a similar situation again. I explained this to my son, and asked him whether he was mad at his first teacher for what she did (whether he judged her); he answered, "Yes." I showed him how he was reaping this judgment again in the new school. We prayed together and he repented of his judgment against both teachers and took those judgments to the cross. Jesus died that my son could be released from judgments and not continue to reap this cycle any longer. The next morning he had no problem with getting ready and going to school.

I had similar judgments as my son. I had had a bad experience in first grade in school and had judged my teacher. The difference between me and my son is that I continued to reap those judgments throughout my school career and a similar negative situation happened every two to three years. I was in my forties when the Holy Spirit opened that up and showed me my judgments against my teachers. After I finished school, those judgments spilled over into other situations with authority figures. Repenting of my judgments made my life a lot easier. All our children have learned about judgments. They usually come to the surface when we use words like always or never—*my sister is always mean to me*, or *he will never share with me*, or *my mom never listens to me, she always wants to be the boss of me,* etc.

Another area that I learned about in prayer ministry training was how we are affected by making vows or promises. We easily and sometimes flippantly make a promise or vow. God knows how bad our reputation is in keeping our promises and that's why He tells us, "But let your 'Yes' be 'Yes,' and your 'No,' 'No.' For whatever is more than these is from the evil one" (Matthew 5:37). We tend to forget these vows or decisions. A vow triggered depression in my life. Every time I had a strong disappointment, the vow kicked in and I was depressed for three days. One time I prayed for a fifteen-year-old girl who hadn't started with her menstrual cycle yet. The Holy Spirit revealed that this girl often said, "I don't want to grow up." I shared with her that in saying that, she was rejecting God's plan for her life to grow and mature. She repented of saying those things and we broke the power of this decision in Jesus' name. Within two weeks, she started her cycle. Words can keep us captive.

It is easy to make foolish decisions because of hurt in the area of relationships. How easily we say things like *I will not allow anyone to come close to me again* or *I won't open my heart to anyone again* when we get hurt. Such decisions can cause devastation in relationships. Because of hurt, a person will put their own decision about what they think they want in a situation above God's will. This is not God's will. It puts them in bondage and steals real freedom from their relationships with others. I am thankful that we can take such foolish decisions to the cross and that their power can be broken so we can walk in the freedom of Christ. If we just flippantly say something like this, it might not take effect, but if we say it with a heart decision and determination, the person's spirit responds and it needs to be broken.

The Holy Spirit Reveals Truth

> "However, when He, the Spirit of truth has come, He will guide you in all truth, for He will not speak on His own authority, but whatever He hears He will speak, and He will tell you things to come" (John 16:13).

The Holy Spirit reveals truth from the Bible to show us the right path. He keeps us on track, through keeping the Word of God before us. Some people benefit by reading one chapter of Proverbs a day for a few months. I easily forget the truths that I read; that is why it is good to go back to the truth of the Word. The Scriptures act as a plumb line to daily bring us into alignment with God's Word.

The Holy Spirit can also reveal truth through a thought, a dream, or a vision. One evening at a small group meeting, one of our friends saw a vision. She saw three of our children run into the arms of God and one hesitated. It was our youngest son who hesitated. I was very concerned about this and started to pray about it. I knew that our youngest son, who was in fifth grade at the time, didn't have the interest in spiritual things that our other children had. I thought it was just because he was more social and into sports. A few days later I had a dream. In the dream we attended a huge conference and I saw our youngest son was not with us. I turned around to look for him and found him with people who he had known when he was much younger. It was a situation in which God was presented as a harsh authority figure.

As I pondered the dream, I wondered if my son had not made a judgment or decision in that situation—that if this is how God was, then he did not want to know a God like that. I shared this with my son and he repented of how he felt in that situation and any judgments or decisions that he had made against God. After this, he changed so rapidly that I had a hard time seeing him in this new light, one in which he pursued God. It was a radical change. I found him reading his Bible without anyone telling him to read it. He was posting Scriptures above his bed that he wanted to focus on. God revealed an issue that kept my son stuck and caused him not to grow spiritually. Judgments and vows can be like rocks in a river. They can dam up the flow. They can prevent us from receiving the blessings that God has for us in situations or they can stop or slow down growth in an area.

Vows or judgments don't affect our salvation. We are saved because we believe in Jesus and receive Him into our lives. Losing our judgments and vows is part of the sanctification or transformation process that the Holy Spirit works in our lives. I was saved, but all the judgments I had against my dad caused my relationship with my husband to be very challenging. When I added the judgments I had against authority figures into the mix, even a quiet introvert like me was challenged in relationships. I was a Spirit-filled Christian who was going to heaven, but my life and close relationships were miserable from time to time. The less baggage we carry the better. "Therefore we also, since we are surrounded by so great a cloud of witnesses, let us lay aside every weight, and the sin which so easily ensnares us, and let us run with endurance the race that is set before us" (Hebrews 12:1).

Discussion Questions: How Does the Holy Spirit Work in Me?

1. "He will convict the world of sin" (John 16:8). Allow a few people to share how the Holy Spirit drew them to Jesus. Write down what drew you to Him below.

   _____
   _____
   _____
   _____

2. The Bible talks about confirming a situation with two or three witnesses, *"by the mouth of two or three witnesses every word may be established"* (Matthew 18:16). The Holy Spirit will confirm a word or change of direction. Discuss possible ways He could do this.

   _____
   _____
   _____
   _____

3. The more important a decision or situation is, the clearer God will speak and confirm it. Discuss the importance of Scripture in making a decision and receiving confirmation.

   _____
   _____
   _____
   _____

4. In Romans 9:1 Paul says, "With Christ as my witness, I speak with utter truthfulness. My conscience and the Holy Spirit confirm it" (NLT). What is the difference between our conscience and the Holy Spirit speaking?

_____
_____
_____
_____

5. Focus on a verse or phrase from the following Scriptures and ask the Holy Spirit to speak to you: Galatians 2:20, Colossians 3:1-4. (Dying to myself does not mean I lose my personality. It means I bring every area under the submission of Jesus Christ—not my will, but His will be done).

_____
_____
_____
_____
_____
_____
_____

Chapter 5: The Holy Spirit Is My Helper

"And I will ask the Father, and He will give you another Comforter (Counselor, Helper, Intercessor, Advocate, Strengthener, and Standby), that He may remain with you forever—the Spirit of Truth, Whom the world cannot receive.... But you know and recognize Him, for He lives with you [constantly] and will be in you" (John 14:16-17 AMP).

The disciples traveled with Jesus as He ministered. They were with Him almost all the time. You can imagine what sorrow and heartache it caused them to see Jesus being crucified. Suddenly their whole world crumbled. Everything changed. Before all this happened, Jesus ensured them that He would not leave them by themselves, but that He would ask the Father to send them a Helper who would always be with them. The disciples didn't understand this at first, but after the outpouring of the Holy Spirit in Acts 2, if people accepted Jesus or were baptized, they asked them: *Did you receive the Holy Spirit?* If not, the disciples laid hands upon them and prayed for them to receive the Holy Spirit. They knew that every Christian needed the Holy Spirit. The apostles lived their lives following the example of Jesus, hearing God's voice and obeying Him.

Who is the Holy Spirit? He is my Comforter, Helper, and Counselor.

"I waited patiently for God to help me; then he listened and heard my cry. He lifted me out of the pit of despair, out of the bog and the mire, and set my feet on a hard, firm path and steadied me as I walked along. He has given me a new song to sing, of praises to our God" (Psalm 40:1-3 TLB).

Discovering the Holy Spirit

When I pray with people, they share their hurt and pain and how others have wounded or rejected them. God's heart is to restore. God is using people to be His hands and feet to minister to people. I have found it to be a huge blessing when others pray and minister to me, but people are not always available to help us. I have learned to turn to Jesus with what is going on in my life. His Spirit is always with me and He can help me to deal with every situation that I face.

When someone gets hurt or is treated unjustly, it can easily turn into a bitterness, resentment, or judgment which hardens a person's hearts and clouds their vision. It goes on to affect how they respond to people. The Holy Spirit is in and with us all the time. He is there when the offense or injustice takes place. If an injustice occurs during childhood, it can affect a person for life unless the Holy Spirit comes and heals it. I have talked and prayed with people who came from abusive childhoods and twenty or more years later, they are still struggling.

God has designed our brains to work in such a way that when we repeat an action several times, we retain it in our memory so that we don't have to learn it all over again and again. When a child learns to walk, the first few steps are wobbly, but after a few weeks the child walks without thinking about it. When we learn to drive a car we have to focus and concentrate on many things, but after a while it becomes second nature. As a one-year-old child I was burned with boiling water and coffee. In my adult years I found that I didn't want to prepare any food that involved deep frying anything in oil. Later I realized my brain had connected the color of the coffee and the hot oil, and that's where the fear came in.

Not deep frying anything in oil isn't such a big deal, but other bad situations can have a debilitating effect on a person's life or relationships. For example, if a woman is sexually abused, she can hold beliefs from that situation. She may have felt trapped. Later when she is married, these beliefs can be triggered. Her husband might sneak up on her and grab her from behind to hug her, and her response might be a frantic, "Leave me alone; don't touch me!" Her current situation is triggering a past memory that looked and felt the same. The problem is we don't remember the memory in that instance; we remember a feeling and don't know why we have that negative feeling, especially because it does not fit the current situation. The woman's husband might not understand how something so simple could trigger such a response. If the woman has repressed her memory, she may not know what is going on either.

In a perfect world the way we learn would also be perfect. We would learn only positive behavior and respond with goodness, kindness, love, and faithfulness to each other. But in a world tainted by sin, we find people with many different kinds of problems rooted in their past experiences. These problems can be triggered because of what happened to them in childhood. They can also have many other causes. Children have attachment disorders because of lack of affection. Hormones or chemicals in the brain that are not in balance can cause problems. Even vitamin deficiencies or food allergies can cause behavioral problems. Other problems or sicknesses can be caused by demonic activity.

There are many different reasons for the challenges people face. This is why we need the Holy Spirit's help to lead and guide us. He knows exactly what is wrong and desires to help us. Let Him lead you in the process of finding answers. Jesus came to give us "beauty for ashes, the oil of joy for mourning, the garment of praise for the spirit of heaviness" (Isaiah 61:3). He came to heal the brokenhearted and to set the captives free—mentally, spiritually, and emotionally.

More than we know, we really need Jesus to help us in this way. It is wonderful when Jesus brings a miraculous breakthrough. God's heart is to give life, to restore, to bring freedom, and to overcome everything that hinders us from living a full life. In my early twenties, I read John 10:10: "The thief does not come except to steal, and to kill, and to destroy. I have come that they may have life, and that they may have it more abundantly." At that time I occasionally struggled with depression and I didn't have a lot of joy in my life. I read that verse and prayed one of those impossible prayers: *God, if it is possible to live an abundant life, please show me how.* I didn't really expect an answer to that prayer, but over the course of the next few years God did what I could not do. He healed my broken heart and the wounds from my past. He set me free from depression and rejection. He applied truth to the many lies I believed about myself.

Discovering the Holy Spirit

Living an abundant life didn't mean that everything always went the way I planned or that nothing bad ever happened, but there was a place of abundance in my spirit where I could live, a place that I stayed connected to God through the Holy Spirit. I don't do it perfectly, but I know how to run to Jesus. I know how to wait and press in, asking the Holy Spirit to give me wisdom about every situation.

God does not always answer instantly. Often a process unfolds in my life—a process that trains me and takes me deeper in the Lord. It usually begins with a choice. I must choose to respond to something that happens, and making that choice sends me to my knees, asking for the Holy Spirit's guidance. For example, someone hurts or offends me, and I feel rejection. I have a choice. My mind can choose to go down the path of *nobody loves me, everybody hates me, woe is me!* or I can choose to allow the Holy Spirit into the process instead. As I go to Him, I ask why this is happening. I ask Him to help me and to comfort me and to guide me. Why do I feel rejected? Is this my problem only, or is it a hurt in the person's heart that caused them to act this way, or a mixture of both? Did I overstep my boundaries? Did I say something I shouldn't have said? He will reveal and show me how it all connects. Then with the Helper at my side, I work through it. I ask forgiveness if I need to do that. I ask the Holy Spirit to wash and cleanse my emotions. Over time this practice has brought me tremendous healing, and I am not as easily hurt or offended anymore. It's the difference between a hasty reaction and a prayerful response.

The Holy Spirit gave me real peace when my mom was very sick before she passed away. It didn't make sense that I should have peace. My mom was having a very rough time. There were times when I felt the burden to pray when I saw my mom was in pain or restless. But I experienced the Holy Spirit's peace and strength in the most difficult times, which I thought was impossible. When the Holy Spirit comforts us, it doesn't mean He takes the situation or pain away. In the crisis with my mom, He gave me peace. After my mom passed away, the trauma of what she went through stayed with me for a while. Every time I remembered it, I released it to God and asked Him to come and heal my heart, to release the memories from me, to wash and cleanse me. I had to do that more than once. I didn't feel anything in particular when

I prayed all those prayers, but six months later on my mom's birthday I thought about her and realized that I was no longer struck with thoughts of the trauma she experienced. All that had been replaced by the Lord with good. Instead I remembered her joy for living.

I've heard the way we carry hurtful and traumatic memories compared to a filing cabinet. The files in the cabinet represent our memories. The hurtful memories are like files pulled up out of place. They are more noticeable. When God brings healing, the file goes into its place and the memory doesn't stir up a lot of feelings anymore. I had many files that were out of place, but God healed them and put them back in place so that they don't hurt anymore. When I look back, I can truthfully say I have grown through every negative situation and become stronger through every adversity.

It is helpful to ask Jesus to bring His perspective about a hurtful situation. One time I was praying with a lady whose mother was verbally abusive. We had a very hard time breaking through the years of pain and abuse. At the end of the prayer time, she suddenly lit up and said, "Now I see it: my mother was afraid she was going to lose my father and she was hurt, and that's why she reacted that way." When the Holy Spirit speaks to us about a situation, everything changes. Knowing the truth set her free. The Holy Spirit had to reveal that to her.

We live in days when families are scattered; divorce and busy lives have done much to damage families. The effect of it can be seen in different ways. In my life it surfaced in codependency, which I was not aware of. I was constantly looking toward my husband to meet all my emotional and physical needs. It was such a burden on him that it pushed him away instead of bringing us closer together. One day when I complained to him about this, he answered that he couldn't meet my expectations. God was supposed to meet those needs. I was surprised by his answer, but it was the best answer he could have given me. I turned my focus to Jesus, and in the process my relationship with my husband improved and I grew in my faith.

When two people get married, they each enter the relationship with a bag of unseen baggage. My husband used to say it is like walking into a mine field. If the landmines are not dealt with it, they will either explode again and again or the two people will learn to avoid them, to not talk about certain issues. My husband used to say he doesn't know where to step. If he stepped on one of those unseen landmines, it ended in an argument. The Holy Spirit helps us recognize and defuse these unseen problems and grow in our marriage.

We live in a microwave and drive-through society where food is served very quickly. God does work through miracles, but changing us to be more like Jesus is a process. We could not handle dealing with everything at once. In God's mercy, the Holy Spirit comes and works little by little, when we are ready, revealing one thing and then helping us deal with it. When I am pressing into God for an answer to a problem, I often pray about it for a couple of days. I take time to think and ponder the situation. Then I go about my day, and the Holy Spirit will suddenly break in with revelation; He will either drop it in my spirit or send me the wisdom I need for the situation through a book or a person He sends my way.

Intercessor

When I pray, I pray to God the Father. I often begin my prayers with Father God or heavenly Father, and approach God in the name of Jesus (John 14:6). The Holy Spirit is the One who helps us pray. I don't always know how to pray for people, but the Holy Spirit knows and He can bring it to my mind and show me what to pray. Usually somewhere in the beginning of my prayer time, I ask the Holy Spirit to show me what to pray or show me what's on God's heart to pray about for that day.

He has often directed me to call my children when they were sick or needed prayer. The Holy Spirit works differently in each of our lives and we need to learn how He speaks and reveals things to us. My husband tends to be the analytical engineer. He is a stable rock. He doesn't make emotional decisions and doesn't get upset easily. Even so, the Holy Spirit gives him wisdom. I think he hears from God so naturally that he doesn't always realize that it is the Holy Spirit. I am the sensitive prayer warrior. God had to heal and restore my emotions, but now I have a very tender heart and often pick up on how other people feel. It took me a while to realize that what I was feeling were not my own emotions. One morning in church I felt this heartache, and I sat there wondering why I was so hurt! What had happened? Nothing! By the end of the service, I noticed a lady two rows ahead of me, crying. I knew then I was feeling her pain and went up to talk to her after the service. She shared that she was still sad about her mother who passed away and she wanted prayer about it. I have learned that not everything I feel is my own. Sometimes the Holy Spirit communicates other people's emotions to me so I can pray for them better. When I continue to pray until I sense a release, I have fulfilled His direction in prayer. This is one of the ways we can partner with the Holy Spirit.

One Friday morning on my way to the house of prayer, I heard news about North Korea on the radio. There were very few people in the prayer room when I got there. I went and stood at the flag of North Korea and began to pray. I felt heartbroken; I cried and prayed for about half an hour for North Korea. When the crying stopped, I went back to my seat. All the negative feelings I had felt were gone and replaced with joy. What had just happened? Earlier that morning, I had been full of joy. After I cried at the flag of North Korea, I felt fine again. Somehow through my tears the Holy Spirit was revealing God's heart, and my tears were part of the prayer for North Korea. Later I learned that such crying prayer is called *travail*. I was praying and crying God's tears for North Korea. I looked up the word *travail* in the Bible, and the first reference is about childbirth (Genesis 38:27). The second reference is connected to hardship and difficulties, a crying out to God (Exodus 18:8)—a crying out to God with tears that brings breakthrough. This is not something I choose to do whenever I want. It is directed by the Spirit of God and is a way of laboring with the Holy Spirit.

There was a time when I experienced this often. When I felt travail come upon me, I went to the staff room, which was usually empty, closed the door and cried and prayed it through. When it was over, I went back to the prayer room again. At the house of prayer, they knew Hermie cried and it was connected to prayer. I am thankful for leaders who could see what the Holy Spirit was doing and did not squelch it. If I didn't obey the Holy Spirit, I felt like I was grieving Him. "Don't grieve God. Don't break his heart. His Holy Spirit, moving and breathing in you, is the most intimate part of your life, making you fit for himself. Don't take such a gift for granted" (Ephesians 4:30 MSG).

The Holy Spirit Is Our Advocate

An advocate fights for a person in court. We have an advocate called the Holy Spirit who fights for us. He is on our side. He sees the big picture and He can see the things that we can't see. He can see the end result; He knows where a path leads. He knows which path in life is the best one to take. That is why it is so helpful to learn how the Holy Spirit helps us, leads us, and works in us. He can draw us away from negative situations and steer us in the right direction if we are open to His leading. When people misunderstand our actions or words, He is the One who fights for us behind the scenes.

Misunderstandings and miscommunication happen easily. We filter the information that we receive through our own experiences and it is easy to see that misunderstandings can happen in that process. But misunderstandings and confusion can also be the work of the enemy. There were times when the Holy Spirit has shown me how to fight with spiritual weapons to take authority in prayer, to command all confusion and misunderstanding to leave a situation in Jesus' name. At other times the Holy Spirit has shown me to take captive vain imaginations (2 Corinthians 10:5). He has also reminded me of Psalm 46:10, "Be still, and know that I am God." At those times, I knew that I needed to be still and focus on Jesus. In each situation we should discern what the Holy Spirit wants us to do. His instructions will bear fruit and bring breakthrough.

The Holy Spirit Encourages and Strengthens Us

Just as we eat food to strengthen and nourish our bodies, there are things we can do to nourish and strengthen ourselves spiritually. When we read our Bibles, pray, worship, spend time with Jesus, go to church, or gather with other Christians, we are strengthened spiritually. As I read my Bible I ask the Holy Spirit to lead and guide me. I ask Him to open the Word and bring revelation. I talk to Him about what I read and ponder the truth of the Scriptures. I am encouraged when I read the truth of God's Word.

One day a young man who is a very good friend of our family called and said the Holy Spirit had placed me on his mind that day. While talking to him he spoke encouragement to me. Up to that point I had not realized how many burdens I was carrying; I felt them lift as he prayed. Afterward I was in awe that God cared enough about me to put me on someone's mind to call and minister to me.

We are the hands and feet of Jesus. The young man who called was being the body of Christ on earth to minister to me. God connects us in a church family. Life is hard and we need family who will be supportive of what we do, encourage, pray, and at times help us. That is the way the early church did it. They gathered together regularly, encouraging one another and caring for one another's needs. The Holy Spirit can also encourage us as we read the Bible. Daily I try to release my cares to the Lord through prayer, "Casting the whole of your care [all your anxieties, all your worries, all your concerns, once and for all] on Him, for He cares for you affectionately and cares about you watchfully" (1 Peter 5:7 AMP). I listen to the voice of the Holy Spirit. I know what a blessing it is to me to receive encouragement from others, so I don't hold back when I can encourage someone else.

Teacher

> "But the Helper, the Holy Spirit, whom the Father will send in My name, He will teach you all things, and bring to your remembrance all things that I said to you" (John 14:26).

The Message Bible describes this relationship beautifully, "I will talk to the Father, and he'll provide you another Friend so that you will always have someone with you. This Friend is the Spirit of Truth. The godless world can't take him in because it doesn't have eyes to see him, doesn't know what to look for. But you know him already because he has been staying with you, and will even be in you!" (John 14:16-17 MSG). I want to say, *Selah, pause and think about that*—a friend like

Discovering the Holy Spirit

Jesus! When I receive the Holy Spirit, I receive a friend like Jesus. This friend lives inside of us. The Holy Spirit is a very practical teacher. His every lesson has a practical application.

In Acts 10 the Holy Spirit worked in Cornelius, a Roman officer who was a God-fearing man. He saw an angel in a vision and the angel told him, "Your prayers and gifts to the poor have been received by God as an offering!" (Acts 10:4). Then the angel told him to send a man to Simon Peter in Joppa and ask him to come to his house. Meanwhile Peter went up on the roof of the house to pray, and fell into a trance and saw a sheet being lowered from heaven. In it were all kinds of animals, reptiles, and birds that were unclean according to the Jewish law. A voice told him to kill and eat of the animals, "'No, Lord,' Peter declared. 'I have never eaten anything that our Jewish laws have declared impure and unclean.' But the voice spoke again: 'Do not call something unclean if God has made it clean'" (Acts 10:14-15 NLT).

Three times this vision was repeated and then the sheet disappeared back into heaven. As Peter was pondering this vision, three men from Cornelius' house knocked on his door. They told Peter that an angel appeared to Cornelius and told him that Peter should come to his house. The next day Peter and other people from Joppa left for Cornelius' house. When Peter arrived, he told Cornelius that it was against the law to come to his house, but God had changed his mind: "I see very clearly that God shows no favoritism. In every nation he accepts those who fear him and do what is right" (Acts 10:34-35 NLT). As Peter was preaching to them, the Holy Spirit fell on the group and all the Jewish believers were amazed that the Holy Spirit was being poured out on them too (Acts 10:1-45).

The Holy Spirit worked in Cornelius' life. He saw a vision of an angel who gave him a message. Peter saw a vision of unclean animals, just before the men from Cornelius' house came to his door. This convinced Peter to go with them even though it was against the Jewish law. The group didn't expect these Roman believers to receive the Holy Spirit, and again they were surprised. As Peter preached the Holy Spirit fell, and he and the others who came with him realized that Jesus didn't only come for the salvation of the Jews. Jesus had come for anyone who would receive Him. They concluded that the group should be baptized. This breakthrough and change of mind was all orchestrated by the Holy Spirit.

The Holy Spirit often teaches me through problems. I have a problem which causes me to seek God for an answer. For example, there was a time in my life when I easily felt rejected. Around that time I had a dream. In the dream there was a house with a tunnel dug by termites. There were no termites in the tunnels, but they must have been there at some point to dig the tunnel, and the tunnel ended in the house right on my dresser. Pondering this dream I realized the house symbolized my life. The dresser was where I looked at myself in the mirror. I understood from the dream that I had a misconception about myself and that it came from outside. In the dream the tunnel had no termites in it, so I assumed that it was a problem that had started in my past, and not recently.

As I prayed, I realized the tunnels represented experiences from my childhood that caused a poor self-image. As I sought God's healing in this area, He directed me to go to many seminars for emotional healing. Over time the Holy Spirit brought healing to hurtful experiences in my past. He also drew me into a deeper intimacy with Jesus. I learned how much Jesus loved me, that God had created me unique, and that I didn't have to be like anyone else. I came to rest in God's love for me. "I have loved you even as the Father has loved me. Live within my love" (John 15:9 TLB).

The Holy Spirit taught me step by step to live in the love of Jesus. When I go through challenging situations, I sometimes feel that I drift away from that place of living in His love. When that happens, I pull out my favorite teachings about Song of Songs and spend some time soaking in those truths again. The Holy Spirit is a practical teacher. He doesn't just give us truth, but teaches us how to apply the truth. There is no other teacher who knows exactly what you need to learn and how. I have grown spiritually and learned a great deal by being open to the teaching of the Holy Spirit.

The Holy Spirit is not a friend who tries to control us. His leading is gentle—so much so that we could easily miss it. We have the choice to ignore or obey. If we choose continuously to resist Him, our hearts

Discovering the Holy Spirit

harden and eventually we don't hear Him anymore. We have the choice of making room for Him or living our lives making decisions in our own strength. The most fruitful way is to involve the Holy Spirit in every area of our lives. That is what Jesus did. The Holy Spirit showed Jesus what His Father desired to do and He followed and obeyed (John 5:30).

It is difficult for me to buy a gift for someone unless I know them well. Recently I wanted to buy my friend's daughter a birthday present. A specific gift came to mind and I went to the store and got it for a great price. When she received the gift, she said, "Just what I needed. It is perfect!" I was astonished and realized it was actually the Holy Spirit who had shown me what to buy. I just didn't realize it at the time. A month later, I missed it again! I was looking for a birthday present for a little girl. She just told me that she had a big art set. I thought maybe I should buy her things that she could use with the art set. When I was in the store I had a craft set in my hand and wondered if I shouldn't buy that. I decided to buy a sketch book and stickers instead.

When the girl opened her gift, she didn't say much and then walked out of the room. Her mom called her and asked her where she was going. She said she was going to put on her happy face. I realized she was disappointed about the gift and I felt bad that I had missed it. She thanked me for the gift. Then she opened her other gifts and her face lit up as she saw craft-oriented gifts. I realized that I should have bought the craft set for her. My mind was so set on what she had told me that I had trouble discerning with my spirit. Later I thought, *I should have asked her mom what she liked.* It was another incident that the Holy Spirit showed me how I put my mind above my spirit. I am still learning. Truly the Holy Spirit cares about even these seemingly small things.

If we allow the Holy Spirit, He will lead us. He can lead us through His peace or by stirring our hearts with a desire to do something. One Saturday morning I had this feeling that my son should go and fill out an application at the fast food restaurant near our house. He wanted to get a part-time job but wasn't driving yet. I asked my husband to take him, but he didn't feel like going. I kept having this feeling that our son should go and asked my husband again. Finally the two of them left. At the restaurant they were out of application forms, but the manager came and said he would quickly interview him right then. After the interview, he told him he had the job and should come in the following Tuesday for training and to fill out the forms. Later I learned that the manager was not there in the afternoons—the time when my son would have gone to apply. By going on that specific Saturday morning, he just happened to be there when the manager was there. It was the exact right timing. I was amazed that this "feeling" I had on the inside was the Holy Spirit stirring me.

God doesn't override our will. That is why people seldom receive audible instructions from God or instructions from angels telling us what to do. He wants us to choose to follow the prompting or tender guidance of the Holy Spirit. As we obey each time and come to know His voice better, we recognize Him more easily. Just as a child comes to recognize the voice of his father and mother, we learn to recognize God's voice. A key in hearing His voice is being obedient to what He tells you to do. One of the ways God trained me was through encouraging others. If I didn't obey Him, it kept bothering me. When I finally shared the encouragement, it was sometimes a bit late. I learned that if the urging I felt was one I could answer immediately, I should not delay. That urging was God's exact and perfect timing. The Bible tells us that the key to intimacy with God is the fear of the Lord. "The secret [of the sweet, satisfying companionship] of the Lord have they who fear (revere and worship) Him, and He will show them His covenant and reveal to them its [deep, inner] meaning" (Psalm 25:14 AMP). This means that we respect and obey God. It doesn't mean we are in trouble if we miss it and didn't realize that He spoke to us. It is the sincere positioning of pursuing Him and intent to hear and obey Him that is most important.

There are Scriptures that have the ability to center our lives. Proverbs 3:6 says, "In all your ways acknowledge Him, and He shall direct your paths." Matthew 22:37 says, "You shall love the Lord your God with all your heart, with all your soul, and with all your mind." I go back to those Scriptures again and again. The Bible brings a clear focus. The things of this life that press on us become less important; they are put in their proper perspective when we read Scriptures like that. As we learn to hear His voice and respond appropriately, we grow in strength and confidence, and He is able to use us more effectively.

He Tells Us of Things to Come

> "That is what the Scriptures mean when they say, 'No eye has seen, no ear has heard, and no mind has imagined what God has prepared for those who love him.' But it was to us that God revealed these things by his Spirit. For his Spirit searches out everything and shows us God's deep secrets" (1 Corinthians 2:9-10 NLT).

God knows the future and He can reveal things to us when we walk with Him. He knows the plans He has for our lives and which choices will bear the most fruit. If we seek Him, He will help us to make the right decisions. Whenever I am in a season of transition or a change of direction is near, I have to seek God for direction. I don't always exactly understand, but sometimes feel unsettled. Sometimes I receive a word from someone or a dream or vision that is helpful. It's like putting a puzzle together. I have different pieces and need to figure out how they fit with the help of the Holy Spirit.

A pastor mentioned that the clearer the Holy Spirit tells us something, the less choice we have. In Acts 9:11 where the Lord told Ananias to go to Straight Street where Paul was and pray for him, the direction is exact and clear. Ananias didn't want to go because Saul persecuted and killed Christians. The Lord told Ananias that He had chosen Paul to take the gospel message to the Gentiles (those who were not Jews). Ananias obeyed and went to Straight Street, and said to Saul, "Brother Saul, the Lord Jesus, who appeared to you on the road as you came, has sent me that you may receive your sight and be filled with the Holy Spirit" (Acts 9:17).

Jesus dealt much more drastically with Saul. Saul was knocked to the ground. A light shone from heaven and Jesus spoke to him and revealed to Saul that he was persecuting Jesus when he persecuted Christians. This revelation caused Saul to make a complete turn around and he became a follower of Jesus too. Paul had a great destiny that would affect many lives and God knew what it would take to bring him to surrender. Paul took the message of Jesus to Asia Minor and Europe. Most of the time God doesn't deal with people as He did with Paul. For a few, this is the only way they will come to Jesus, but most people turn to Jesus when they are in a desperate situation or looking for answers.

God confirms what He speaks to us. He can do it in many different ways. Often He uses His Word. He gives a Scripture to confirm. Sometimes someone will share a similar message to confirm a word from God. In early 2014 I had a dream. In the dream I was in the house of prayer and I saw a cylindrical tube that had wheat falling through it. It reminded me of Joseph storing grain for the coming famine in Egypt in Genesis. That same week I read prophetic words about an end-time harvest of souls. I thought the dream I had might represent the ingathering of a harvest of souls. The next day I read the Scripture, "Do you think the work of harvesting will not begin until the summer ends four months from now? Look around you! Vast fields of human souls are ripening all around us, and are ready now for reaping" (John 4:35 TLB). I immediately realized God was giving me a confirmation of what He had been speaking to us about harvest. This is a prayer strategy. God was directing me to pray to release laborers to reap this harvest. We need the Holy Spirit to be our Teacher and Friend in our lives. I do not want to live life any other way.

Discussion Questions: The Holy Spirit Is My Helper

1. Give some examples of how the Holy Spirit has been or can be your Comforter, Counselor, Helper, Intercessor, Advocate, Strengthener, Teacher, and Friend.

   _____
   _____
   _____
   _____

2. How do you involve the Holy Spirit in a problem or hurt you have? Discuss the following:

   He knows everything; nothing you can tell Him will shock Him.

   The blood of Jesus is available to wash you clean.

   Jesus has forgiven you, so ask Him to help you to forgive others.

   He knows who has hurt you. Even though He knows it, you can tell Him; but don't just tell Him, go the next step and ask Him to remove the hurt, to actually heal the hurt.

   _____
   _____
   _____
   _____

3. The Holy Spirit reveals truth to us. Often He does it through a Scripture. He can do it through a situation you are walking through that brings revelation too. He can also speak through a friend, a book, and many other ways. If you can think about a situation in which He spoke truth to you in one of these ways, share it with the group.

   _____
   _____
   _____

4. "That He may remain with you forever" (John 14:16 AMP). This is the key to living a successful life as a Christian. There are times when we walk by faith and times when we feel as though the Holy Spirit is more present than others. The truth is that He is always with you. Share some thoughts that could be helpful to others about when you walked through times when it felt like He was not there.

_____
_____
_____
_____
_____
_____

5. Focus on one of the words or phrases in the following Scripture and allow the Holy Spirit to speak to you. Write down what He says.

> "And I will ask the Father, and He will give you another Comforter (Counselor, Helper, Intercessor, Advocate, Strengthener, and Standby), that He may remain with you forever—the Spirit of Truth, Whom the world cannot receive.... But you know and recognize Him, for He lives with you [constantly] and will be in you" (John 14:16-17 AMP).

_____
_____
_____
_____
_____
_____

Chapter 6: The Holy Spirit Has a Ministry for Everyone

"For as we have many members in one body, but all the members do not have the same function, so we, being many, are one body in Christ, and individually members of one another" (Romans 12:4-5).

My mom was a lady full of life and spirit. She got excited about the little things in life. It gave her joy when her roses bloomed or she found the first fig on her young fig tree. When she walked into a store, she would be in conversation with somebody in the store within five minutes. I am more introverted than she was. I find it difficult to walk up to a stranger and start a conversation. I admired my mom who could so easily talk to people and had such joy for living. I wanted to be like her. Trying to be like her took tremendous effort. Eventually I realized God had created me differently. There are areas I can grow in, but I don't need to be like my mom.

God has given each person a gift mix and wired them in a specific way to fulfill the purpose He has for their lives. "Just as our bodies have many parts and each part has a special function, so it is with Christ's body. We are many parts of one body, and we all belong to each other. In his grace, God has given us different gifts for doing certain things well" (Romans 12:4-6 NLT). If we know how God has fashioned us and the gifts and talents He has given us, we can flow with them. When we try and do something that is not according to our gift and talents, it is hard work and takes a lot of effort.

The spiritual gifts outlined in Romans 12:4-10 are the focus of this chapter. Just as we have natural gifts, we have spiritual gifts that need to be developed. We are born with some gifts, but can also receive spiritual gifts later in life. We can receive gifts in many ways—by impartation when people pray for us, through dreams, as well as through personal prayer. One time I had a dream about receiving a gift. When I opened the box, there was a glass jug that looked like a measuring cup, but it had no measurements on it. After that I started to walk in greater discernment. Around that time I had often prayed and asked for an increase in discernment. I have read many biographies of people who ministered in healing. It is a common theme in their stories that they experienced a life-changing event when the Holy Spirit came and empowered them for ministry. But we don't have to wait for that to happen. There are times when God calls us to seek Him more. We have the Holy Spirit in us to help us pray for people. If we don't have a specific gift, it doesn't mean we cannot prophesy or pray for the sick. Our connection with the Holy Spirit allows all believers to hear God's voice and tell others what He is saying. When we pray the Holy Spirit is right there and He can touch someone. We can also ask God for spiritual gifts or to bring increase to an area. He wants to flow through us.

Prophecy

> "God has given each of us the ability to do certain things well. So if God has given you the ability to prophesy, then prophesy whenever you can—as often as your faith is strong enough to receive a message of God" (Romans 12:6 TLB).

We live in the days that Joel 2 prophesied about when God has poured out His Spirit, and is still pouring out His Spirit, upon people. It started when the Holy Spirit moved powerfully in Acts 2 and Peter said this was what the prophet Joel had prophesied about, but God didn't stop there. He is still pouring out His Spirit. The prophecy said that the sons and daughters would prophesy, old men would dream dreams, and the young men would see visions. God wants to speak to all, young and old. He will reveal Himself to all who seek Him, young and old (Jeremiah 33:3).

Hermie Reynolds

To prophesy is to hear God's voice and to speak what He is saying. The New Testament tells us, "But he who prophesies speaks edification and exhortation and comfort to men" (1 Corinthians 14:3). If we stick to these guidelines, prophecy is safe. It can become messy when we leave the path of edification, exhortation, and comfort. One of our sons was part of a ministry that had prophetic teams. People fly from all over the world to visit this ministry and its prophecy rooms. My son shared how wonderful it was to see the way God encouraged people through the words they received. He saw what a great need there was for Holy Spirit encouragement. He said the Holy Spirit often spoke words about the destiny of a person or encouraged them in their relationship with God.

As I went through training about hearing God's voice and prophetic ministry, I learned there should not be any element of control in a word. God gives us a choice in what we want to do with our lives, so when we give someone a word from God it should not be a controlling word. We should not say things like, "You should change your job or move to a new city." The ministries I have been trained through do not prophesy dates, marriages, babies, or job changes. What I hear from God is filtered through my mind. Because of that, I can make a mistake or hear something wrong. I should not share anything that could control someone's destiny. That is very dangerous. We are each accountable to God for the decisions we make. God will not accept the excuse that we followed the word of a prophet. We need to hear from the Lord on our own for directions in our lives.

A prophetic word from God can be a huge blessing. When I received a word about writing, I could decide whether I wanted to pursue it or not. Because other doors closed at that time, I decided to give it a try. God encouraged me along the way, and I received two similar words about writing halfway through the task.

I really want to hear God when I listen for a word for someone. If I don't hear anything specific, I pray a blessing over them. It helps to be in a team of two or three people. Usually one person receives something, and as he shares the other one gets a word too.

Discovering the Holy Spirit

Start by encouraging people in normal situations. Our pastor encourages people in a very natural way. He goes up to a child in one of his children's basketball teams and tells him, *I see how you encourage the team, keep it up.* A person doesn't need to be prophetic to do this, we just need to take the focus away from ourselves and observe what is happening around us. I have been blessed by my friends calling me at times, telling me the Lord has laid me on their hearts and encouraging me.

God speaks to some people through pictures (visions) and to others through a word or sentence or through impressions. Some people see pictures in their mind—this is a seeing gift like the seers in the Bible—and others hear words and have a hearing gift, which is similar to how the prophets received their revelation in the Bible. "Now the acts of King David, first and last, indeed they are written in the book of Samuel the seer, in the book of Nathan the prophet, and in the book of Gad the seer" (1 Chronicles 29:29). There are also people who will say, "It feels like God is saying...." I often get impressions like that; it is not a picture or words. It could be a memory of something that happened to me and I know God has a message to the person that is connected to that. Sometimes I have a sense the person is struggling with finances. I didn't see a picture, God didn't reveal anything to me in words, but there is just a knowing that this could be what the person is struggling with. I ask them if they struggle with their finances. If the person says yes, I pray over their finances. There are other ways God can speak to us too, and I will share more of those in a later chapter.

Children can also hear God's voice. I have practiced this with children. First, we pray and ask God for a word or a picture for someone else. If the picture is negative, then I instruct the children to pray the opposite of it; I also taught them to pray for protection and bless the person. One child saw a picture of a shark for someone, so we prayed God's protection over that person and canceled every assignment of the enemy against them. I help them to understand that God's purposes and God's love are stronger than anything else, so they need not be afraid of anything. I help them see that God wants them to work with Him as a team to pray for others.

Prophecy can be a great blessing. People already know their sin. It is so much more powerful to release a person's destiny through a word, to call them forth out of what they are stuck in, into what God has for them. Prophetic words release the hope that God has for us and bring forth His plan in the midst of our struggles. They give us hope and bring encouragement. They stir us to go forward into the plans God has for us and help us leave behind that which does not produce life.

If God reveals something bad that will happen to a person, He is revealing it so we can pray and stop it so it will not happen. There have been times when friends of ours had dreams or words from God that something bad would happen. One friend woke up in the middle of the night from a dream in which our son was under a truck. She knew it was a call to pray.

The next day I was cleaning the filter of our pool. Our two-year-old son was with me. I suddenly wondered why it was so quiet. Where was he? When I turned around, I saw that he had fallen in the pool and was under the water. I jumped in and got him out. He was fine. I believe my friend's intercession that night turned around plans that the enemy had to take our son's life. Every time there has been a warning from God that something bad was going to happen, we were able to turn the situation around through prayer and it didn't happen. "The thief does not come except to steal, and to kill, and to destroy. I have come that they may have life, and that they may have it more abundantly" (John 10:10). If you are serving God, expect that He has good plans for you!

If I see something and I am not sure if it is from the Lord, I take my thoughts captive in the name of Jesus unto the obedience of Jesus Christ. Because I often see pictures or visions from the Holy Spirit, I have found that I have to be careful what I watch on television or in movies; otherwise I see visions that are not from the Holy Spirit. I once heard a story about a young boy who saw angels. His dad told him to ask the angel why he couldn't see them. The angel said his dad had seen too much evil. Our eyes are gates to our soul. "The lamp of the body is the eye. If therefore your eye is good, your whole body will be full of light" (Matthew 6:22).

My son told me that after he worked in the restaurant in the evening, he had to wait a little bit before he went to bed to just relax and unwind; otherwise he had crazy dreams. Everything that happened that night was still stirred up in his spirit and he dreamed about it.

What we experience and go through is often reflected in our dreams in symbolic language. God does speak to us through dreams, and as we grow in Him we can learn to distinguish which dreams are from Him, which are from our own spirit and connected to what we experienced during the day, and which are from the enemy.

Serving Others

> "If your gift is serving others, serve them well" (Romans 12:7 NLT).

Oh, how we need those with this gift. Servanthood is the gift that can greatly bless leaders. If there is an absence of servanthood, the work will not get done. The leader or leadership team that receives strategy from the Lord needs people to bring that plan to fruition. I have been a mom for a long time and the cleaning, cooking, and laundry never ends. I serve my family with pleasure. We have been part of the leadership team in a church plant. The first year of setting up equipment and taking it down after the service was hard work. Even now that the church has a building, it needs to be cleaned; someone needs to buy supplies, and my husband often makes the coffee Sunday mornings. No leader can be successful without those who are called to serve with him. In Acts 16:14-15 we read about Lydia from Thyatira who sold purple cloth, which was very expensive in those days. As she was listening to Paul's preaching, God opened her heart and she was baptized. She opened her home to Paul and Silas, allowing them to stay there. Salome, Mary Magdalene, Mary, and other women traveled with the group that followed Jesus' ministry and took care of them (Mark 15:40-41).

When God called Moses, he responded that he couldn't speak well (Exodus 4:10-14). God gave Aaron as a helper to him. Later Jethro, Moses' father-in-law, gave Moses sound advice. He asked him who the people go to with their disputes. Moses said they came to him. Jethro told him it was too big a burden to carry all by himself, and that he should appoint elders who could help him. Moses did that and it helped to lessen the load he carried (Exodus 18:13-26). The New Testament talks about elders and deacons. First Timothy 3:1-13 gives guidelines for deacons and elders. James 5:14-15 also reveals that the elders prayed for the sick, "Are any of you sick? You should call for the elders of the church to come and pray over you, anointing you with oil in the name of the Lord. Such a prayer offered in faith will heal the sick, and the Lord will make you well. And if you have committed any sins, you will be forgiven" (NLT).

After the Last Supper, Jesus washed the disciples' feet. This was their last time together. What a powerful final message, "If I then, your Lord and Teacher, have washed your feet, you also ought to wash one another's feet" (John 13:14). When the disciples asked Jesus who was the greatest in the kingdom of heaven, Jesus called a child and told the disciples that whoever humbled himself like this child was the greatest in the kingdom (Matthew 18:1-4). Little children are humble and innocent. I once taught first graders. They believed that what their teacher said was law. They wanted to please their teacher and were very teachable. In the kingdom of God, humility and being teachable are the best ways to position ourselves before God, whether we are helpers or leaders. The Bible tells us that God resists the proud (James 4:6). He hears the desire and prayers of the humble (Psalm 10:17). He teaches the humble His ways (Psalm 25:9). It is wise to walk in humility no matter what position we are in. I have heard the word *servant-leader*—that is a good description of how we need to be. If a leader is humble enough to be able to serve, he will lead well.

Teaching Others

"If you are a teacher, teach well" (Romans 12:7 NLT).

Our first learning opportunities take place in the family we grow up in. There we learn our basic life lessons, and they will shape our lives. In a family, learning takes place spontaneously. Moms and dads are the first informal teachers of their children. They are also the people with the greatest influence and ability to teach and impart to their kids; their influence lasts longer than any other teacher. Our families and childhood experiences shape our lives. To have a good family who loves each other is the greatest gift a child can receive. It will shape the child's future and build strong foundations in their lives.

As we grew, we all had teachers. Each person can tell you the name of a teacher who influenced them. One summer our daughter took a college geography class. She enjoyed the class very much and said the teacher must have enjoyed teaching this class because he even taught it in the summer, and it was very interesting. A teacher who is called to teach loves to teach, and when they teach those who are listening they learn too.

A characteristic of a teacher is the ability to teach systematically, starting at point a, then b, and then c. They like order and can organize material in a way that makes it easier to understand. When you listen to a good teacher, their topic just opens up and understanding comes. I have been blessed to listen to great Bible teachers, and when you find such a teacher you feel as though you cannot get enough. I just wanted to hear more and more. Usually I bought their books or teaching CDs or listened to them online. One can learn much from a great teacher.

Usually people have one gift they're strong in, but may walk in other gifts too. We find pastors who are great teachers, or pastors who are very prophetic, as well as pastors who are strong evangelists. It is wonderful that God has created each one of us uniquely and each person's gifts are a blessing where they serve, whether it is teaching at school, in a college, as a pastor, or as a Bible teacher.

We read about people's response to the teaching of Jesus, "And they were astonished at His teaching, for His word was with authority" (Luke 4:32). The words of Jesus had the authority of heaven behind Him. He spoke in the power of the Holy Spirit. Paul realized that he needed the power of the Holy Spirit resting on his words to convince people who Jesus was: "And my speech and my preaching were not with persuasive words of human wisdom, but in demonstration of the Spirit and of power, that your faith should not be in the wisdom of men but in the power of God" (1 Corinthians 2:4-5).

Encouraging Others

> "If your gift is to encourage others, be encouraging" (Romans 12:8 NLT).

Hermie Reynolds

One of the foundational teachings that I received as a young Christian was about having an intimate relationship with God. Around the same time I learned that "the fear of the Lord" meant to obey God immediately, and that delayed obedience was the same as disobedience. This referred to situations that could be accomplished immediately. This helped me grow in my relationship with God and in hearing His voice. The Holy Spirit does not continue to speak to us when we know we are walking in disobedience. For many years the Holy Spirit trained me—through promptings to write an encouraging note, card, or e-mail to a person. I was surprised how people responded to them. Often I was told that the Scripture or encouragement I had written was exactly what they needed at exactly the right time. Sometimes they just needed to know that God loved them. Eventually God connected me to intercession groups at the churches we attended or ministries in town. I often received a Scripture or dream or vision for the church which was mostly for the purpose of prayer. I acted on what the Holy Spirit showed me as He directed. Sometimes I simply prayed about a situation; other times I spoke with someone about what God had shown me.

We need encouragers in the body of Christ. When the encouragement is Holy Spirit-inspired, it is the right word that the person needs at the right time. Don't be afraid to start there. A lady, who travels in the body of Christ and teaches people to hear God's voice, tells people that all she heard from God for the first year was, "God loves you with an everlasting love"; she was faithful to deliver that message, and over time God opened up more words. When she shared that testimony, it encouraged me that it was possible for me to hear God's voice for others too.

Encouragement is so needed in the days we live in. Our church is in a college town and we meet many young people. I am surprised to see how many of them do not know that their life has value and purpose. I look at them and can see great destiny, but they need someone to encourage them and declare God's truth over them so they can come into what God has for them. We can all grow in the area of encouragement, whether it is our specific gift or not.

Giving

"If it is giving, give generously" (Romans 12:8 NLT).

This is a wonderful gift and I am sure one we all would like to have. Jesus said, "It is more blessed to give than to receive" (Acts 20:35). One summer one of our sons went to the Bahamas to help with a children's camp; it was a very blessed time for him. He saw how God touched and changed the lives of children in three days. He came back and told us there would be more opportunities to go to other countries to do camps. Then he said he didn't know if he would be able to go, because he had to work and could not take all summer off. It made me sad to think that a lack of finances could limit God's work. Jesus said, "The harvest truly is plentiful, but the laborers are few" (Matthew 9:37). When I see someone who wants to be a laborer, I feel provision should not be a problem. We can greatly advance the kingdom of God by giving into ministries that are bringing forth good fruit.

God gives each of us some ability to give to others. Whether He has gifted you with much or with little, we can all give something. The more we possess, the bigger the responsibility we have to be a good steward. God has big plans and resources and people are needed to accomplish these plans. Those who work in the marketplace or own businesses have a crucial part in advancing the kingdom. Without the necessary finances those who are called can't go. Each person—wealthy or not—has a place in God's bigger plan. If you support one missionary, you are part of sending someone into the harvest field. We each need to see where God is calling us to help or sow financially.

I love to give when I know God is in the giving. We cannot help everyone and there are many needs on the earth, but each one of us can help someone. I have found that through the years God has connected me with different people who need what I can give. For some it was food, for some clothes, for others time and help. The motives of our hearts are important, "So let each one give as he purposes in his heart, not grudgingly or of necessity; for God loves a cheerful giver" (2 Corinthians 9:7). When the Holy Spirit is in the giving, there is grace to do it.

Hermie Reynolds

Leadership

"If God has given you leadership ability, take the responsibility seriously" (Romans 12:8 NLT).

Leaders have a large responsibility. They are responsible for a group of people. When my husband was promoted at his job, he felt the responsibility of the position. He suddenly had a say in whether a person got a job or did not get the job, whether someone stayed or was let go from the company. To me it was a blessing to see that he felt the responsibility and didn't take it lightly. I was glad that he realized that the decisions that he made affected families; he considered each situation seriously and prayerfully. He had genuine concern for the people he worked with.

When my husband and I became parents, our life changed dramatically. We truly wanted to take care of our daughter, no matter what. She had colic the first three months and cried a lot. Suddenly I hardly had time to dress myself. My mom was working and couldn't help me. My husband helped in the evenings, often rocking our daughter when she cried at 5 a.m. I was exhausted and at the end of my wits, but there was no other option; everything we did was focused on trying to help this little baby. Gladly her colic lasted just three months. After that, she was the sweetest baby. Children changed our lives forever. Suddenly life wasn't just about us anymore, but we made decisions in the light of what would be best for the whole family.

When a leader has genuine care and concern for people, they are the best leaders. If a leader just wants to build their own ministry, people will not be as committed and relationships will suffer. The book of Acts says, "And the apostles preached powerful sermons about the resurrection of the Lord Jesus, and there was warm fellowship among all the believers, and no poverty" (Acts 4:33-34 TLB). The apostles were the leaders of the early church; later they appointed deacons because their workload became too much. I personally think God is raising up team ministry today. The burden is not as heavy when a leader has a good team.

An insecure leader can find it difficult to let go and allow others to share the burden and the work. Sometimes they might have an attitude of *this is my business* or *my ministry*. When a leader operates as a mother or father, the focus shifts and it becomes: *how can I help the people who work for me or are in this ministry with me to become the best at what they do and fulfill the purpose God has for their lives?* The focus shifts from w*hat can they do for me?* to *how can I help them?* The last thing Jesus did after He and His disciples had the Passover meal was to wash the disciples' feet. He showed them a living example of servant leadership.

Leaders can lead a group of people to relationships and communities that are a blessing, or they can scatter the flock and people get hurt. When a leader does not walk in godly character, the flock gets hurt. Look at a picture of a shepherd and his sheep. If the shepherd, the leader, is taken away, the sheep scatter. That is why we need to pray for our leaders. "Therefore I exhort first of all that supplications, prayers, intercessions, and giving of thanks be made for all men, for kings and all who are in authority, that we may lead a quiet and peaceable life in all godliness and reverence" (1 Timothy 2:2). Leaders have the ability to protect the people they lead; then the people live in peace. Leaders who are greedy or self-centered cause harm and suffering to come to the people. Good leaders can be a tremendous blessing to those they lead. The Bible sets a high standard for the character of leaders (Titus 1:6-9). A leader can influence many people. If a leader makes poor decisions, those who work with the leader suffer too.

When our children became teenagers, we learned to slowly let go and help them become more independent. When they reached the required age and wanted to get a temporary license, we encouraged them to do so. They went through driver's education and when they could drive well and had put in the required hours, they took the driver's test. At first we just allowed them to drive short distances to school and back, before we trusted them to take longer trips. It was a blessing to see how they matured and started to take responsibility for their lives. I think a parent provides the foundation for a child to become independent, to have their own relationship with God and live in dependence on God. Even when we prepare for it, when they finally flew out of the nest, I wasn't fully prepared. When one or our sons was in his second year in Bible school, I was expecting him to come home for the summer like he usually did. He casually answered. "I don't know, Mom. I think I want to go on a missions trip to Thailand." He was following the Holy Spirit, and I knew I had to step back and allow him to make his own decisions. Today I am just happy and thankful whenever I can see them.

Mercy

> "And if you have a gift for showing kindness to others,
> do it gladly" (Romans 12:9).

What a beautiful gift. I have not found many people who were just kind to me for no reason at all. Our youngest son has a tender merciful heart. He always gave me a hug when he left for school or basketball practice. He had a heart to help people in Third World countries with resources and training. We really need those with hearts of mercy.

Now that my children are grown, I pick up a friend's daughter from school once a week, and I teach art to another friend's kids. Because I have been a mom for twenty-four years, I enjoy being able to spend some time with kids. It is a blessing to them, but a joy to me. They're such great kids. There are many ways that we can volunteer a few hours and make a difference in someone else's life. Some have a heart for the poor and collect coats and shoes for children when winter comes. Others help with the local food pantry or donate gifts around Christmas time. I think we all can give something whether we have the gift of giving or not. The Bible says, "And remember the words of the Lord Jesus, that He said, 'It is more blessed to give than to receive'" (Acts 20:35).

Love Wraps the Gifts

> "Don't just pretend to love others. Really love them.
> Hate what is wrong. Hold tightly to what is good. Love
> each other with genuine affection, and take delight in
> honoring each other" (Romans 12:9-10 NLT).

Discovering the Holy Spirit

Most people quickly recognize when others are not sincere. It is much better to serve one another from a heart of love. I know I don't have enough love in my heart, but Jesus does. A missionary who has planted many churches in Africa said her biggest challenge is spending enough time in the presence of God every day. When she does, she is filled with God's love and compassion for the orphans in the ministry. Being filled with the love of Jesus is central to our ability to minister.

Spending time in the presence of God in the prayer room in an atmosphere of continuous worship and prayer was part of the Bible curriculum in the school our sons attended. Before our kids went to this school, we attended an informational meeting. The president of the school said that the kids do not only learn head knowledge, but as they spend time in God's presence their personal human spirit expands. I have seen much spiritual growth in their lives because of this. It reminds me of Ephesians 4:15: "We take our lead from Christ, who is the source of everything we do. He keeps us in step with each other. His very breath and blood flow through us, nourishing us so that we will grow up healthy in God, robust in love" (MSG). I am very encouraged to see God raise up young men and woman whose priority is to seek Him first and then to do what He has called them to do.

When Jesus was asked what the first commandment was, He answered, *"And you shall love the Lord your God with all your heart, with all your soul, with all your mind, and with all your strength"* (Mark 12:30). He said the second commandment was to love our neighbors like ourselves (Mark 12:31). Notice that Jesus said *love*. He did not say *serve* the Lord Your God with all your might. We get tired if we work hard. Love will go to greater lengths. One who loves will do everything they can to please the one they love. It is much better to serve God and others because we love Him—because we have the love of God in our hearts.

In Acts 6 the apostles were overwhelmed by their duties in taking care of the people and preaching and teaching. They chose seven people full of faith and the Holy Spirit to help them. Stephen was one of those who was chosen (Acts 6:2-6). Stephen did great miracles and signs among the people. One day men from the Synagogue of

Freedmen started to debate him. They could not resist the wisdom and understanding the Holy Spirit gave Stephen (Acts 6:8-10). It is encouraging to read about ordinary men and women who lived extraordinary lives because they served the Most High God, knew Jesus, and had a relationship with the Holy Spirit.

Discussion Questions: The Holy Spirit Has a Ministry for Everyone

1. Read through the different gifts and check those that are your strongest gifts. Give opportunity to share your thoughts about this.
   - ☐ Prophecy: This refers to speaking into the lives of others with insight from God.
   - ☐ Serving: This includes making food, cleaning, organizing, gardening, building, repairing things, and much, much more.
   - ☐ Teaching: Babies, children, youth, or adults all need teachers.
   - ☐ Encouraging: Everybody needs encouragement.
   - ☐ Giving: The gospel will not advance without people giving money, time, and resources.
   - ☐ Leadership: Without a leader, there is chaos. Servant leadership: The disciples learned from and followed Jesus when He showed them how to lead. Jesus washed their feet to teach them that a leader should serve.
   - ☐ Mercy: Mercy draws us into the presence of God. From that intimate place, where we receive God's mercy, flows the mercy to minister to and help others.

2. Write down a few thoughts about what the Holy Spirit showed you from this chapter. Give a few people the opportunity to share.

_____
_____
_____
_____
_____
_____

3. Share some stories about a great teacher you had and why that person was a great teacher. What makes a person a great teacher? Write down the things you think of.

_____
_____
_____
_____
_____

4. Mercy: It is easier to give someone food and clothes than to get involved and help them grow spiritually and emotionally so they are able to live a better life. We cannot make decisions for others, but the goal of mercy is not just to give people food or clothes, but to help them reach the place where they regain their dignity in living and have a sense of being loved by Jesus. Jesus wants to call them to a higher place. We are part of that transformation. Discuss.

_____
_____
_____
_____
_____

Discovering the Holy Spirit

5. Read 1 Timothy 3:1-12. We all are leaders and teachers, even if it is just in our own homes. Choose a phrase or verse from the passage to focus on and let the Holy Spirit speak to you about it.

_____
_____
_____
_____
_____
_____
_____
_____
_____

Chapter 7: The Holy Spirit Releases Training and Equipping Gifts

> "Some of us have been given special ability as apostles; to others he has given the gift of being able to preach well; some have special ability in winning people to Christ, helping them to trust him as their Savior; still others have a gift for caring for God's people as a shepherd does his sheep, leading and teaching them in the ways of God" (Ephesians 4:11 TLB).

The ministry of the pastor is the fivefold ministry gift with which we are most familiar. My favorite pastors through the years have been those who were great father figures. They displayed God, the Father's heart, and cared for people. Just like a father loves, protects, and leads his children, helping them become responsible adults, it is a blessing if pastors have the heart of God for those under their care spiritually. A pastor can be a very positive and encouraging influence in a person's life. This is why the enemy often targets pastors. He knows if he can take out the shepherd, the sheep will scatter and many will get hurt. We need to pray for our governmental and spiritual leaders (1 Timothy 2:1-3).

Our middle son had an opportunity to do an internship at a house of prayer. He felt led to do the night watch (12 to 6 a.m.). The leader of the group asked him what he would like to do that he hasn't done before. He replied he would like to try and lead a worship set. He plays three instruments, but usually doesn't sing. He was assigned to lead a weekly 4-6 a.m. worship time. I could tune in to the webstream to listen to my son. When that alarm clock rang, I thought only a parent would get up in such a tired state and make this sacrifice. But I listened and enjoyed the time of worship. The interludes that he played during that time were beautiful. I encouraged him to continue, and it was a blessing to him that his mom gave up her sleep to listen to him. That's what parents do.

I wanted to encourage my son, but how much more does God want to encourage and cheer us on? He can do it in many different ways, but He often does it through our friends or through the leaders we work with. I have a few friends who have the gift of encouragement, and it is a great blessing when I receive a word of encouragement from them at just the right time. Leaders are a blessing as they encourage those they train and equip. It is wonderful to hear someone say: *I see you're growing in the Lord. God hears your prayers. He hasn't forgotten you. I see your heart for Him.* "Let everything you say be good and helpful, so that your words will be an encouragement to those who hear them" (Ephesians 4:29 NLT).

Look at the Scripture at the beginning of this chapter. It uses the word *some*. God has appointed *some* in the body of Christ as leaders. These leaders comprise a small percentage of the body of Christ. God released the grace and the gifts to them to train and equip the rest of the believers to do the work of the ministry. "Their responsibility is to equip God's people to do his work and build up the church, the body of Christ. This will continue until we all come to such unity in our faith and knowledge of God's Son that we will be mature in the Lord, measuring up to the full and complete standard of Christ" (Ephesians 4:12-13 NLT). The result of the ministries of the apostles, prophets, evangelists, pastors, and teachers is to bring the body of Christ to maturity and to strengthen our faith that we will stand strong in the truth and not be easily shaken or lose faith when we face difficulties.

When we receive Jesus as our Savior, we are transferred from the kingdom of darkness to the kingdom of light; we receive heavenly citizenship (1 Peter 2:9). We are born into this new kingdom spiritually immature. We lived in the kingdom of darkness, pleasing ourselves, living life from our souls and minds. This new kingdom operates in a different realm. We need to learn how to live and walk in fellowship with the Holy Spirit. It is a process of walking, yielding, and obeying step by step, submitting my thoughts and plans to the lordship of Jesus. It doesn't mean I ignore my mind or can't think rationally.

Hermie Reynolds

It was difficult for me to learn how to hear God's voice at first because He spoke to me differently than the way my friends heard Him. It was like learning a foreign language. God gives me impressions, dreams, signs—sometimes even in magazines or the Internet. He goes on to confirm what He is speaking. When we did an outreach once, the Holy Spirit showed those who were praying that the prodigals were returning to God. Just a few days after that, I read a word and it confirmed exactly what we were hearing from God that evening.

When I hear a word, I need to discern whether it is God speaking to me or just my own thinking or desire. Then I must discern whether or not the word is for me, for the purpose of prayer, or something I should share with the leadership or the body of Christ. If it is something that could bless another person and I have the means to do it, then I don't spend a lot of time trying to discern whether it is God or not. As I have responded to Him, I have grown in my ability to hear His voice. He sometimes brings a person to my mind so I will pray for them or I have the thought to contact a friend and encourage them. The Holy Spirit is the best Friend and Helper you can get, because He is always on the lookout for your best interest as well as looking at ways that others can be blessed and ministered to through you.

At first we are taught, and eventually we teach others. That is the natural cycle of growth. Just as we have to eat regular meals to grow physically, there are things we can do to help us grow spiritually. Growth doesn't happen automatically. Growth occurs when we attend church, fellowship with other Christians, spend time reading the Word, pray, and worship. It is wise to make time in our schedules to seek God.

I have heard the fivefold ministry explained according to the five fingers on our hands (see text box on next page).

We cannot separate these fingers—they are part of the hand. God is bringing the hand, the fivefold ministry, into a fuller functioning level in the church. We need every ministry gift working together to come to maturity. A hand with just three fingers doesn't function as well as a hand with all five. Each gift is helpful. The body of Christ will function best if the fivefold ministry gifts work as God called and purposed them to do.

> The thumb is the apostle. We need the thumb to have a solid grip. Apostles are strong leaders and often have the ability to walk in all five of these functions.
>
> The pointing finger is the prophet. Prophets point the way, bring clarity about situations, and give direction.
>
> The middle finger is the evangelist. Evangelism is the outreach ministry of the church; it shares the gospel message as far as it can reach.
>
> The ring finger is the one that holds the wedding band, a symbol of our commitment to our spouse. This finger refers to the ministry of pastors who are committed to their flock. Pastors are the ones who are concerned about the welfare of their people and watch over them so that no wolves come and harm them.
>
> The pinkie finger is the teacher—small but not insignificant. The teacher builds truth upon truth. Good teaching transforms us. The work of the teacher is often invisible, but as we grow and mature, we see the work God has done as a result of good teaching.

The fivefold ministry is sometimes referred to as the office gifts, meaning a person who walks in them often receives a title. We call our pastor by that title. A woman who is considered an apostle once said that people don't often call her by the title "apostle" but she functions as one. The Living Bible reads "special ability as apostles" (Ephesians 4:11). God gives a special ability or grace to a person to function in the fivefold ministry gifts. And these are not only ministry gifts, but also equipping and training gifts, given for service to the body of Christ.

Apostles

Paul begins his message to the believers in Rome with, "From Paul, a bond servant of Jesus Christ (the Messiah) called to be an apostle, (a special messenger) set apart to [preach] the Gospel (good news) of and from God" (Romans 1:1 AMP). An apostle is a messenger, a delegate, one who is sent forth with orders.[9] The ministry of an apostle is appointed by God. It is a gift given by God. In Romans 1:10-11, Paul is praying to visit the Romans to impart spiritual gifts and strengthen and encourage them. Paul traveled and preached the message of Jesus Christ. He planted churches and visited them again and again to encourage and strengthen the believers in their faith.

An apostle is a leader who is filled with godly wisdom; they often walk in the other four office gifts as well. They preach, teach, evangelize, and walk in the power of the Holy Spirit. Often apostles have a traveling ministry of teaching, preaching, and doing miracles. The apostle can be an overseer who plants churches and gives wise counsel to leaders. This is the report of the apostles in the book of Acts: "And through the hands of the apostles many signs and wonders were done among the people" (Acts 5:12).

Jesus is the chief Cornerstone and Head of the church. The Bible says the foundation upon which the church is built is the apostles and the prophets (Ephesians 2:20). Several years ago I had a vision of a house built upon a rock (Matthew 7:24-25). What was significant about this house was that the foundation was sunk into the rock; even the bases of the walls were inside the rock. I knew that house would be strong and able to withstand any storm. In my vision, the apostles and prophets couldn't be seen. They were well hidden in the rock, Jesus; but they provided the strength for the house to be strong. The apostle Peter wrote about us, "you also, as living stones, are being built up a spiritual house" (1 Peter 2:5).

In South Africa, people build brick homes. The outside walls are interlocking double bricks that are held together by cement. This makes the walls very strong. The tightly knit unity in the Spirit that we share is like those walls. "Behold, how good and how pleasant it is for brethren to dwell together in unity!" (Psalm 133:1). "Now protect them by the power of your name so that they will be united just as we are" (John 17:11 NLT). Here is another picture of a body functioning together:

---

9. Thayer and Smith, "Greek Lexicon entry for *apostolos,*" The KJV New Testament Greek Lexicon, Accessed March 1, 2015, http://www.biblestudytools.com/lexicons/greek/kjv/apostolos.html.

> "Instead, we will lovingly follow the truth at all times—speaking truly, dealing truly, living truly—and so become more and more in every way like Christ who is the Head of his body, the Church. Under his direction, the whole body is fitted together perfectly, and each part in its own special way helps the other parts, so that the whole body is healthy and growing and full of love" (Ephesians 4:15-16 TLB).

Even though the apostles and the prophets were actually invisible in my vision, they made the house strong. The rest of the house was clearly seen. The church needs to be built up and strong in the days we live in. It is not a time to sit on the fence or waver in our faith. We are part of a spiritual house that shines in a dark place. Our light needs to be bright if we are to help others and bring them to the Lord.

Prophets

Elijah is a well-known prophet from Bible times. He delivered messages from God to the king and confronted the priests of Baal in a head-on confrontation to show who really knew God. Baal's priests cried out to their god for hours to set the wood on fire, but no fire came down from heaven. Elijah had water poured on his altar three times until it was sopping wet. Then He cried out to God and fire came from heaven to ignite the wood and consume the sacrifice (1 Kings 18:25-38). The result: "Now when all the people saw it, they fell on their faces; and they said, 'The Lord, He is God! The Lord, He is God!'" (1 King's 18:39).

Jeremiah was called to be a prophet to the nations even before he was born (Jeremiah 1:5). In the Old Testament they had a school for the prophets (1 Samuel 10:5-10). In the New Testament, Agabus was shown by the Holy Spirit that there was going to be a great famine in the world (Acts 11:28). Other prophets are also named, "Now in the church that was at Antioch there were certain prophets and teachers: Barnabas, Simeon who was called Niger, Lucius of Cyrene, Manaen who had been brought up with Herod the tetrarch, and Saul" (Acts 13:1-2).

There were also women prophets. Deborah the prophetess was a judge in Israel. People came to her for help in making decisions (Judges 4:4-5). Miriam, the sister of Moses, was a prophetess (Exodus 15:20).

Isaiah's wife was a prophetess (Isaiah 8:3). In the New Testament, Anna was called a prophetess. She was widowed at a young age and spent her life in the temple, praying and fasting. Anna didn't have a visible or large ministry. She was in her eighties when Jesus' parents brought Him to the temple. The Holy Spirit showed her that Jesus was the Messiah. She told everybody that she had seen the child, the Deliverer, the One they had been expecting (Luke 2:36-38). Philip the evangelist had four daughters who prophesied (Acts 21:8-9).

Prophets are clear voices for God and they speak what God tells them to say. Zacharias prophesied over his son, John the Baptist, that he would be a prophet, "The voice of one crying in the wilderness: 'Prepare the way of the Lord'" (Matthew 3:3). John grew up in the wilderness until God's appointed time came for him to be released into his ministry. The prophet carries a responsibility to speak for God. The character of a prophet should reflect God's heart for the people. If a prophet's character hasn't matured or if the person is wounded, it can taint the prophet's words. John the Baptist's message was very clear: "Repent, for the kingdom of heaven is at hand!" (Matthew 3:2). This is typical of the prophet's personality; they tend to see situations black and white. The prophet often receives revelation from God about how to pray for certain situations. During the Egyptian revolution in 2011, a woman prophet released a word that the enemy's plan was that many people would be killed, but God wanted to bring awakening in the Middle East. This was a helpful word to me. It gave me direction about how to pray for the Middle East.

People feel the need to know what the future holds; some go to psychics or fortune tellers to tell them what will happen. The difference between a psychic and a prophet is that the psychic receives their revelation from a demonic spirit and the prophet receives their revelation from the Holy Spirit. In Acts there is a slave girl who had a spirit of divination who earned a lot of money for her owner by fortune telling. She followed Paul and those with him and annoyed them by continuously proclaiming that they were servants of the God Most High (Acts 16:16). God said we should not have any idols before Him (Exodus 34:14). He forbids divination, fortune telling, and any practice that uses a different source than Him to find out knowledge. Those practices bring a person under a curse. God wants to protect people (Deuteronomy 11:26-28; 18:14).

Discovering the Holy Spirit

In 1 Samuel 28:3-20 King Saul inquired of God about a situation and didn't receive an answer. Then he asked a medium to conduct a séance for him so he could talk to the prophet Samuel. The message Saul received was that God had left him and that the whole army of Israel would be defeated the next day. God did not respond to Saul because of his disobedient heart. Consulting a medium made everything worse. If he had repented of his sins and turned back to God, the story could have ended differently. In 2 Chronicles 18:20-22, God allowed a lying spirit to influence his prophets. Why? King Ahab didn't really want to know the truth. We cannot knowingly allow idols in our hearts and expect God to speak to us. If we want to hear from God, it is vitally important that we keep our hearts clean. We should approach Him as Jesus did: *Father, not my will, but Your will be done.*

Some prophets travel in the body of Christ and give personal words to individuals, releasing their destiny. Hearing God's plan for them brings life to people. A word from God can release destiny, healing, deliverance, restoration, encouragement, and breakthrough. Some prophets have the ability to recognize sin. A prophet should be careful how they deliver a message. One prophet mentioned that in the beginning of his ministry, he shared the words just as he received them. Fewer and fewer people came to his meetings. He learned to prophesy to the heart of the person instead of the exact words he received. For example, if God showed him that a lady sitting in the back was a prostitute, he didn't say that to her. If he did, she would run out the door! Instead he spoke to the heart issues, saying she had been wounded and rejected by people. This opened her heart to receive prayer.

When Jesus told the woman at the well that she had had five husbands, there was no one else there. Jesus didn't embarrass her in front of other people. What He told her convinced her that He was the Messiah and her message changed a village. A woman who travels and teaches about the prophetic shared that she had experienced very few times in which God gave her a direct and negative word for a person. Once she had met a drug dealer and God told her to tell him that if he didn't turn his life around, he was going to die. This is the exception. Usually prophecy speaks forth the potential of a person and not how sinful they are. It gives people hope that they can change; prophetic words and prayers can unlock destinies and break chains.

There are also those who are called to the office of prophet; this grants them a higher level of authority. In Amos 3:7 it says that prophets know the secrets of God, "Surely the Lord God does nothing, unless He reveals His secret to His servants the prophets" (Amos 3:7). One prophet I know told me the foremost call of a prophet is prayer. A prophet can be called to a region, city, or nation, and some travel internationally and release words over nations. God reveals His plans to them and they release them and give directives about how to pray.

God gave Israel prophets to reveal His plans and what was on His heart for them. "I will raise up for them a Prophet like you from among their brethren, and will put My words in His mouth, and He shall speak to them all that I command Him" (Deuteronomy 18:18). In the Old Testament prophets were held to high standards. Verse 20 tells us that if a prophet spoke and he was not commanded by God to speak, he should die. Moses is referred to as a prophet who knew God face to face (Deuteronomy 34:10), "and at God's command he performed amazing miracles which have never been equaled" (Deuteronomy 34:12 TLB). Prophets are drawn to spending time with God, because it is in their personal intimate relationship with God where they receive revelation. God speaks to His friends.

We all need to hear from God. We need His guidance and wisdom for our work, church, neighborhood, and city. Each of us has a sphere of authority, and we need to hear from God what to do and how to pray over that sphere. He might send a prophet to confirm what He is already speaking to us, but we should not depend on prophets to give us words. If God wants to speak to you through a prophet, be open and pray about the word, but our responsibility is to seek God for ourselves. God sometimes speaks to me through my friends and will give them a word to give me. It is always a blessing to receive an encouraging word through one of my friends. I often use those words to pray forth God's will. If you receive a word, you need to discern whether it is something the Holy Spirit is stirring in your heart to pray about and pursue. When the Holy Spirit was poured out in Acts 2, He opened the way for every believer to be able to prophesy, because we all have the Holy Spirit.

I heard God's voice as a young Christian long before I knew about prophets or prophecy. Hearing His messages was just part of the natural flow of my relationship with God. Sometimes He gave me words to encourage others, which I shared. When I was obedient to share what the Holy Spirit spoke to me, people were blessed and encouraged by the words. The prophet is simply doing this on a bigger scale. He hears God for a nation, a region, or a church group. Prophets can be great mentors, teaching believers to hear God's voice and encouraging them to prophesy.

Prophecy does not change doctrine; the Bible determines doctrine. Never make decisions based upon one prophetic word. A prophetic word should never contradict the truth in the Bible. Let the Holy Spirit guide you. God wants to speak to you. Often a prophetic word will be a confirmation of what you already know. If we have preconceived ideas, we can misinterpret a word. It is important to ask God to speak and confirm His words in other ways. Anyone can make a mistake. Follow the inner witness of the Holy Spirit over a prophetic word. If the inner witness of the Holy Spirit agrees with the word and you feel you have other confirmations, then go ahead. Timing is important too. Often God's timing is much slower than we expect.

A word from a prophet can have a tremendous impact. In 2009 I received a prophetic word about writing books. I never considered such a thing! This happened during a time when the ministries I worked with were in a transition and there wasn't much opportunity for me to teach like I had before. My kids were all grown and I had time on my hands. I felt like all my plans were falling apart, and then I received that word. I did not know what else to do with it so I started to write a Bible study. As I looked back in my journals later, I found an entry of a dream that I had written a book. I had the dream about a year before I received the word. But it felt like such an impossibility that I didn't pay any attention to it. God actually tried to tell me, but I ignored it. The prophetic word brought life to me in a time of transition when I did not know what to do; it also brought a huge change of direction. The right word at the right time can have a powerful impact.

Sometimes prophets see natural disasters that might happen. When a prophet releases a word like that, it is a call to pray. One day I was praying from Jonah. In the beginning of Jonah, God is saying that He is going to destroy the city, "for your wickedness rises before me; it smells to highest heaven" (Jonah 1:2 TLB). We know the story. Jonah tried to run away from that mission and found himself in the belly of a whale. Three days later he was spewed out by the whale and obeyed God and went to Nineveh. He preached to them that God was going to destroy Nineveh. To his surprise the people turned from their sin, fasted, and repented. "Who can tell? Perhaps even yet God will decide to let us live, and will hold back His fierce anger from destroying us" (Jonah 3:9 TLB).

This is a lesson to us—even though Jonah delivered the words of God's coming judgments, yet, perhaps, God could hear their prayers and hold back His anger. We see the result, "And when God saw that they had put a stop to their evil ways, he abandoned His plan to destroy them, and did not carry it through" (Jonah 3:10 TLB). After this the prophet was depressed. Everything he said was going to happen didn't happen. God is a gracious Father and He gives mercy time and again. We too should pray in the face of coming judgment. At the same time, we must not be ignorant and think God will continue to bless a nation if there is no repentance, and people continue to destroy and disrespect the life God has created.

The ultimate purpose of the prophet is to reveal God's restoring redemptive purposes on the earth. Malachi prophesied of a prophet who would "turn the hearts of fathers to the children, and the hearts of children to their fathers" (Malachi 4:6 NLT). John the Baptist came and when people repented from their sin, they received a spiritual heart transplant. God took out their stony hearts and gave them tender hearts. This still holds true today—the purpose of a prophet is restoration. Pioneers in deliverance and emotional healing ministries also often have prophetic gifts.

How the gift functions is most important. There are people who function in the marketplace as prophets. They receive direction and strategies for businesses. Those who are on the cutting edge of social issues are often prophets, "voices in the desert." More people function as prophets than the few who are recognized as being in the office of prophet.

Evangelist

The ministry of the evangelist is well known. There have been evangelists who have caused millions to turn their hearts and lives to Jesus. An evangelist travels and preaches about the good news of Jesus Christ. Philip was chosen to be a deacon in the book of Acts to help with the distribution of food among the widows (Acts 6:5). He eventually became an evangelist (Acts 21:8). Most people are familiar with the work of an evangelist. They usually travel from city to city and preach to large crowds, telling people the good news of who Jesus is. A person who has this gift easily shares the message of Jesus wherever they go. I met such a man once. Wherever he went he shared about Jesus—in the store, at the dentist—everywhere he went, he talked to people about salvation. We are all called to share the good news of Jesus Christ in our daily lives. Second Timothy 4:5 is an encouragement to keep on sharing the truth. Verse 4 talks about a time when people would not want to hear the truth, "But you should keep a clear mind in every situation. Don't be afraid of suffering for the Lord. Work at telling others the Good News, and fully carry out the ministry God has given you" (2 Timothy 4:5 NLT).

There is a description of the ministry of the evangelist in Acts 8. Philip went to Samaria and preached about Jesus. Multitudes witnessed evil spirits being cast out and the paralyzed being healed (Acts 8:5-8). The miracles attracted people to the meetings where the good news was shared. The evangelist should equip the body of Christ for more evangelism. There are many evangelism trainings available in the body that can be very helpful in teaching how to share Jesus with others. The most important factor is how we live. If our words and our lives don't agree, people will not want our Jesus. Start praying for those who you want to share the gospel with. The Holy Spirit will prepare their hearts and they will be more open to listen. Build relationship with them; this will lead to opportunities to either share more about Jesus or allow you to ask them if they need prayer for anything. Let this flow naturally and listen to the Holy Spirit. Another option is to ask, *Do you know Jesus?* or *Do you know if you will go to heaven if you die?* Even if someone says no, they don't need prayer, they will soon find themselves in a situation where they realize they need prayer, and the Holy Spirit will use your words.

They are like seeds sown in their lives. Listen to the leading of the Holy Spirit. God knows and cares about people and their needs.

Pastor

The ministry of a pastor is compared to a shepherd leading his sheep, taking care of the flock. In John 10 we find the parable of the shepherd caring for his sheep. In different places in the Bible we find God or Jesus depicted as a Shepherd. The Shepherd takes care of His flock. He knows them by name. He protects them from wild animals. A pastor has a heart for his people too. He knows where they are spiritually and what they need to grow in their faith. He protects them from being led astray, and he points the way to God as the One who can meet their needs. In Jeremiah 3, God says Israel is like a faithless wife; again and again they forsook God for idols. God is saying if they will return to Him, He will restore them and give them leaders according to His own heart, "who will feed you with knowledge and understanding" (Jeremiah 3:15). The ministry of the pastor is beautifully illustrated in this verse: "still others have a gift for caring for God's people as a shepherd does his sheep, leading and teaching them in the ways of God" (Ephesians 4:11 TLB).

A pastor's job is not easy. The enemy often stirs up areas of the flesh in people—murmuring, a critical spirit, gossip, or slander—and then he finds a way to use it to bring strife, confusion, and miscommunication in churches and ministries. A leadership team that is grounded in their faith and filled with the Holy Spirit's wisdom and understanding is a tremendous help to a pastor.

Jesus had the heart of a shepherd: "But when He saw the multitudes, He was moved with compassion for them, because they were weary and scattered, like sheep having no shepherd" (Matthew 9:36). The pastors who have made the biggest impression on me were those with a father's heart. They were like a father in the spirit to their people. We need fathers in the body of Christ. Fathers don't only teach; they also impart a sense of love, security, stability, and safety, which enables a person to come into the fullness of God's plan for their lives.

Discovering the Holy Spirit

Teachers

Jesus was called *Rabbi*, which means teacher. "This man came to Jesus by night and said to Him, "Rabbi, we know that You are a teacher come from God; for no one can do these signs that You do unless God is with him" (John 3:2). In Bible times, rabbis traveled from city to city to teach. They had a following of disciples who stayed with them all the time. They learned by observing and doing what their teacher did as well as by accumulating knowledge. The title *rabbi* was a term of respect, just like we call someone pastor or doctor. Paul said of himself, "I was appointed a preacher, an apostle, and a teacher of the Gentiles" (2 Timothy 1:11).

In Isaiah 28 it says God gave the farmer wisdom to know when to plant crops and when and how to harvest: "The Lord of Heaven's Armies is a wonderful teacher, and he gives the farmer great wisdom" (Isaiah 28:29 NLT). Isaiah 30:20 says, "And though the Lord gives you the bread of adversity and the water of affliction, yet your teachers will not be moved into a corner anymore, but your eyes shall see your teachers." God's promise to Israel was that He would be with them even in adversity, and that is His promise to us too. The Holy Spirit will be with us, lead, and guide us if we follow and obey Him (John 14:26).

Teachers are judged with greater strictness by God (James 3:1). A teacher can impact a student's life greatly. I can still remember some of the great teachers I had in school. I also remember the bad experiences I had with some teachers. Jesus said that if anyone led a child astray, it would be better for that person if a millstone were hung around his neck and they were drowned (Matthew 18:6). If we see teaching kids from this perspective, we will teach them truth. A teacher can teach truth or lead someone astray. The truth that a teacher releases can set people free. Jesus said we will know the truth and the truth will set us free (John 8:32).

A teacher enjoys studying. He can organize material in a way that it is easier to learn and understand. "Keep this in mind: The Teacher was considered wise, and he taught the people everything he knew. He listened carefully to many proverbs, studying and classifying them" (Ecclesiastes 12:9 NLT). We need great teachers in schools, in colleges, in training, and in church to teach and train us for the work of the ministry. "The Teacher sought to find just the right words to express truths clearly" (Ecclesiastes 12:10 NLT).

The Purpose of the Fivefold Ministry Gifts

Those who function in the fivefold ministry gifts should strengthen, encourage, build up, and teach the body of Christ. Recently a friend told me that he read that Chinese believers say if they go to prison for their faith they see it as training to mature as a Christian. Trials and difficulties either cause a person to lose their faith or surrender to God. Surrendering brings spiritual growth and strengthens faith. As we grow and mature in our faith in Jesus and knowledge of God, the body of Christ will come into greater unity. "Instead, we will speak the truth in love, growing in every way more and more like Christ, who is the head of his body, the church. He makes the whole body fit together perfectly. As each part does its own special work, it helps the other parts grow, so that the whole body is healthy and growing and full of love" (Ephesians 4:15 NLT).

I opened this chapter with Ephesians 4:11; it says, "He has appointed some." "Some" are called to these ministry functions. So what about the rest of us? Each of us has a gift. What you really enjoy doing is a hint to where your gift lies. Some people are naturally neat and organized. They usually do well in business and administration. Our son took a job one summer and he found himself in a situation where they were relabeling and repackaging gloves in a factory. He came home and pointed out the inefficiency of the way it was done. He actually made a few suggestions to the group, and his changes made it easier for them to do the job. It was frustrating for him to do the same thing over and over, and he found himself seeing how things could be done in a different way. Repetitive, assembly-type work was not for him. This is not what he was called to do for the rest of his life.

If you are trying to identify your gifts and callings, take note of what you enjoy. Find your strengths. Look at the opportunities God has placed in front of you. We live in a time when people will be needed for jobs that do not yet exist. If we look at how technology is advancing, we can see this is true. Those who hear the voice of God will be needed—in every business, company, government, school, and hospital.

Discussion Questions: The Holy Spirit Releases Training and Equipping Gifts

1. Name the fivefold training and equipping gifts. Share if you know someone who walks in these gifts.

   _____
   _____
   _____
   _____

2. Do you think God had a plan for your life even before you were born (Jeremiah 1:5; Psalm 139:14-16)? Write down a few things that are strengths that God has given you. (For instance, are you a good planner, creative, organized, strategic, or a peacemaker?)

   _____
   _____
   _____
   _____

3. Write down areas that you see as weaknesses. (Is it hard for you to speak in front of people, answer telephones, listen to others, serve, visit the sick or the elderly?)

   _____
   _____
   _____
   _____

4. As you look at your strengths and weaknesses, do you think you are doing what God has created you to do?

_____
_____
_____
_____
_____

5. Read 1 Corinthians 12:12-27, choose a Scripture or phrase to focus on, and ask the Holy Spirit to speak to you. Write down what He says.

_____
_____
_____
_____
_____

Chapter 8: Can I Receive the Gifts of the Spirit?

> "But the manifestation of the Spirit is given to each one for the profit of all: for to one is given the word of wisdom through the Spirit, to another the word of knowledge through the same Spirit, to another faith by the same Spirit, to another gifts of healings by the same Spirit to another the working of miracles, to another prophecy, to another discerning of spirits, to another different kinds of tongues, to another the interpretation of tongues" (1 Corinthians 12:7-10).

As Christians we have the indwelling Holy Spirit who is our Helper, Friend, and Guide. He is helping and changing us to become more like Jesus. But there is another aspect of the work of the Holy Spirit. He is also the One who empowers us for ministry. We are born with particular gifts. A person can have the call to be a prophet or have a prophetic gift even before birth. We read that Jeremiah was called to be a prophet even before he was born (Jeremiah 1:5). We can also receive the empowering of the Holy Spirit for ministry later in life. Jesus received the empowering of the Holy Spirit to do miracles when He was baptized (Matthew 3:16). Before Jesus ascended into heaven He told the disciples to wait in Jerusalem for the Holy Spirit. They waited for forty days and in Acts 2 we read what happened when the Holy Spirit was poured out upon them. They received a supernatural empowering to bear more fruit when that happened.

A gift can also be imparted. Paul said in Romans 1:11, "For I am yearning to see you, that I may impart and share with you some spiritual gift to strengthen and establish you" (AMP). Paul laid hands on people, "And when Paul had laid hands on them, the Holy Spirit came upon them, and they spoke with tongues and prophesied" (Acts 19:6). The Holy Spirit can be transferred by the laying on of hands. We can also receive an impartation from those under whose ministry we train. During my foundational years as a Christian, I listened to a lot of teaching by a lady who spent several hours a day studying the Bible. I can see that this influenced me in a positive way to have a strong foundation in the Word of God. When I went through prophetic training and learned that God can speak to us through dreams, there was an increase in that area in my life. Someone once compared it to rubbing shoulders. When we rub shoulders with a Christian who has a gift in a certain area, some of that can rub off on us. Over time we grow and change. I have grown to walk more in God's wisdom; I didn't always have that.

When I sense God is taking me into a new season, I spend additional time in His presence, asking Him to release the empowering and equipping that I need for that season. I can spend time with Jesus and feel great, but it doesn't last all week. I need to spend time with Jesus daily and allow the Holy Spirit to fill me. First Corinthians 12 outlines different ways the gifts of the Holy Spirit can manifest. We can all walk in these gifts and ask God to increase them in our lives. Some people might walk more strongly in some of the gifts, but the gifts are for everyone. God has something for you.

Word of Wisdom

We all need wisdom. Just to have knowledge doesn't bring us far if we don't know how to apply it. James 1:7 tells us if we need wisdom, "let him ask of the giving God [Who gives] to everyone liberally and ungrudgingly, without reproaching or faultfinding, and it will be given him" (James 1:7 AMP). That's easy enough—just ask. I have learned to seek wisdom continually, bringing it before God again and again. Sometimes He brings it through Scripture or I find it in a book. Other times He speaks to me through a friend or even a person I do not know well. He also speaks through dreams or mental pictures. When I receive a dream or a vision that stays with me, I think and pray about it for a couple of days. Why was it a red car and not a yellow car? Why was it a truck and not a car? Why am I walking or riding a bicycle? Where am

I going? Is the dream about me or is it about someone else? Am I just observing in the dream or am I part of it? Sometimes, even after a day or two, the Holy Spirit will reveal what it means. Sometimes I will get only one piece; it is like pulling on the loose yarn on a jersey. As I pull on it, it unravels. In the same way, when I receive part of the revelation, it slowly unfolds. "My mouth shall speak wisdom, and the meditation of my heart *shall give* understanding" (Psalm 49:3). I have too many dreams to pay attention to all of them. I write down all the dreams I remember. I only spend time on a dream when I feel there is something that God wants to reveal to me or I feel the need to understand it.

Once I gave a businessman a word. I told him he walked in the gift of wisdom in his work and that it came so naturally that he didn't recognize when it was him and when it was the Holy Spirit speaking. I just suddenly knew that! I was surprised. Later as I considered it, I realized there were times when I knew what to do, and it was the Holy Spirit but I didn't realize it. God uses everything. He uses the knowledge we gain through studying, reading, and learning in life. If we receive supernatural wisdom on top of that, it can be really helpful. Many things that I have learned in school, through books, or in life have helped me to make good decisions in my life, but I keep myself open to receive Holy Spirit wisdom. There are many times when I just don't know what is best. It seems like either path is fine. God knows which one is the best, so ask, ask, and ask again. He will guide you in the way you should go.

Wisdom and understanding go together. When we receive wisdom, then the situation opens up and we usually know why something happens and what to do. "Wisdom is found on the lips of him who has understanding" (Proverbs 10:13). True wisdom does not make someone prideful; it brings humility. When I receive God's wisdom I see how wise He is compared to what I was thinking. "When swelling and pride come, then emptiness and shame come also, but with the humble (those who are lowly, who have been pruned or chiseled by trial, and renounce self) are skillful and godly Wisdom and soundness" (Proverbs 11:2 AMP). We need a humble, open heart and an attitude of dependence upon God to receive from Him.

Discovering the Holy Spirit

Word of Knowledge

A word of knowledge is a specific insight into something that we cannot know with our natural mind. Jesus told the Roman officer that because of his faith his servant was already healed, and he could return home at peace (Matthew 8:13). How did Jesus know? The Holy Spirit told Him. Philip went to tell his friend Nathaniel and told him they had found the man who the prophets in the Old Testament prophesied would come. Nathaniel went with Philip and when Jesus saw him, He said, "Now here is a genuine son of Israel—a man of complete integrity" (John 1:47 NLT). Nathaniel was surprised and told Jesus they hadn't met before and asked how it was possible that Jesus knew this about him. Jesus told Nathaniel that He saw him when he sat under the fig tree. Jesus had seen Nathaniel in a vision in His mind and the Holy Spirit had revealed this to Him about Nathaniel. Nathaniel responded, "Rabbi, you are the Son of God—the King of Israel!" (John 1:49 NLT). Jesus received information from the Holy Spirit about Nathaniel which He couldn't have known in the natural.

Often a word of wisdom and knowledge flow closely together. Part of the word might be knowledge and the other part wisdom about how to implement it. Some people physically feel pain and know it is God telling them that someone needs healing in that area. For example, a sense of knee pain not your own could be a word of knowledge that someone in the meeting needs prayer for healing for a knee problem.

Faith

My African-American Christian friends come to mind when I think about faith. Many of them have a strong gift of faith and had ancestors who had to strongly believe that God would deliver them. I can learn much from them in this area.

The first gift of faith we receive from the Holy Spirit is the gift of having faith for salvation. To come to the belief that Jesus died for me and gives me eternal life when I receive Him as my Lord and Savior is a work of the Holy Spirit. God often uses difficult circumstances in people's lives to open their hearts to receive Jesus. When they realize that they're not in control of everything that happens in their lives, they begin to look for answers. All through this process, the Holy Spirit is working in their lives. He sends people to speak to them, encouraging them, witnessing to them, or telling them God can help them.

When I am in a situation where I need to pray for someone and don't have the faith for what I am praying for, I ask God to release the faith I need. I have at times operated in a gift of faith when praying for a city; I just felt the faith to ask certain things from God for that city. This happens when I pray for people too. Recognize what God gives you faith for. There have been times when I led a two-hour prayer and worship session for our city and I didn't have a lot of faith that day. To prepare I spent fifteen to twenty minutes of the prayer time focusing on Scriptures that declare who God is. These truths built my faith. Focusing on God's capabilities gave me faith that He could help our city, and then I could better lead in prayer. Reading and hearing the Word of God (Romans 10:17) is a primary way to bolster our faith. Faith is important; without faith we cannot please God (Hebrews 11:6).

Gift of Healing

God can give a person a gift of healing. If a person has the gift of healing they will often connect with a healing ministry or travel as a healing evangelist. If you have an intimate relationship with God and allow His Holy Spirit to work in your life, and God releases a gift of healing or miracles to you, just follow and obey Him the same way you do in your personal relationship with Him. The gift might take you into ministry over large groups of people. It doesn't matter whether we are called to minister to crowds or one on one. Walking in relationship and obedience to God doesn't change.

We live in the time when every Christian can walk in a greater measure of the Holy Spirit. We can pray in faith for the healing of the sick. If we do not have this specific gift it doesn't mean we can't pray for someone anyway. I am obedient to pray when someone who needs healing comes my way and the Holy Spirit stirs me to pray for them.

Jesus released healing by speaking it out. Consider these verses: "And He said to her, "Daughter, your faith has made you well. Go in peace, and be healed of your affliction" (Mark 5:34); "But say the word, and my servant will be healed" (Luke 7:7); "And He cast out the spirits with a word, and healed all who were sick" (Matthew 8:16). Jesus followed and obeyed the Holy Spirit as He healed people. Sometimes he touched the eyes of a blind person to receive sight (Matthew 20:34). One time He put spit on his hands and then put his hands on a blind man's eyes. The man's sight was gradually restored. Jesus had to put His hands on the man's eyes a second time before the man could see (Mark 8:23-25).

For personal healing I have learned to press into God. Some of the problems I experienced in my body were linked to eating too many processed foods. God educated me about changing my diet so I could be healthier. In 2012 I attended a meeting of a lady who saw a lot of healings during her meetings. My arm had been hurting for about three months. Looking back I think I probably had a hairline fracture. It didn't hurt so much that I felt like I should go to the doctor, but it would get better and then I would pick up something heavy and then it hurt again. When I went to the meeting I had to sit in the overflow area. It was packed and I saw little possibility to receive prayer. As the lady started to call out different conditions God was healing, I laid my hand on my arm and asked Jesus to heal it. I continued to release God's healing power into my arm. It felt a lot better after the meeting. I could have done that at home! But I also knew that when the Holy Spirit is present to heal, and there is a strong presence of God in a meeting and an expectation for healing, I could connect to the Holy Spirit and ask Him to heal me even if I didn't get prayed for by the speaker. My arm felt a lot better and within a few days the pain was gone and didn't return again.

Working of Miracles

Something miraculous happened to the disciples when the Holy Spirit manifested through a wind and tongues of fire in the upper room in Acts. They received an empowerment to walk in the miraculous. Miracles can be instant healings, but they also refer to the multiplying of the fish and loaves (Matthew 14:14-21) or the calming of the storm (Mark 4:39). In Acts 3:6, Peter and John went to the temple and saw a lame man sitting there begging for money. Peter told him, "'Silver and gold I do not have, but what I do have I give you: In the name of Jesus Christ of Nazareth, rise up and walk.' And he took him by the right hand and lifted him up, and immediately his feet and ankle bones received strength. So he, leaping up, stood and walked and entered the temple with them—walking, leaping, and praising God" (Acts 3:6-8). This is supernatural Holy Spirit power. Jesus walked in it. The disciples walked in it, and some of the believers walked in it. Stephen was full of the Holy Spirit (Acts 6:5) and Philip who became an evangelist did great signs and wonders (Acts 8:6-13).

A missionary from Africa once shared how she started to pray for the deaf. She continued doing it until she saw deaf people's ears open. Then she had faith to pray for the blind, and now she sees blind people healed. Miracles attract people to Jesus in countries where they haven't heard the gospel. When Peter preached in Acts 2, he said, "People of Israel listen! God publicly endorsed Jesus the Nazarene by doing powerful miracles, wonders, and signs through him, as you well know" (Acts 2:22 NLT). Miracles are a public endorsement by God that Jesus is still alive. It is the power of the Holy Spirit operating through healing and delivering people, drawing them to Jesus. Even if we don't have the specific gift of miracles, we can pray and ask God for a miracle when someone needs one. The Holy Spirit is enough for whatever situation we face and He can help and move through prayer. He is available to us at any time. We live in a microwave-minded society; people just want to press a button and solve their problems. God does that at times. He is a miracle-working God; but there are other times when He says, *your problem can be solved by changing in some other way instead.* Change can be instantaneous or incremental. Either way, press into Him. He has the answer.

Prophecy

We have explored the ministry of the prophet earlier. We can all prophesy and hear God's voice. The words "prophet" and "seer" are first found in the Old Testament: "Now the acts of David the king, first and last, behold, they are written in the book of Samuel the seer, and in the book of Nathan the prophet, and in the book of Gad the seer" (1 Chronicles 29:29). The word *seer* comes from the Hebrew word *ra'ah*, which means to see or perceive.[10] A seer receives revelation from God in visual form. They see a picture or a series of pictures like a short movie playing in their minds. Some call it the imagination. God uses our imagination. But not every picture we see in our minds comes from God. As we grow in hearing His voice, we can discern when it is God and when it is not.

When I am not sure about something, I put it on the shelf. If the revelation was from God, He will repeat it and bring confirmation. The word *prophet* comes from the Hebrew word *nabiy'* which means spokesman, speaker, those who prophesy.[11] A prophet receives revelation from God in auditory form. It is seldom the audible voice of God. Most of the time, they hear the soft inner voice of the Holy Spirit. There is another group of prophets. My son call them "the feelers." They could fall under the seer's definition of "to perceive." They will give a word like this, "I feel God is showing me...." They get impressions or sense what God is saying. Some people are more auditory, others see, and still others feel what God is communicating. The Holy Spirit can communicate to us in many ways. Learn how He communicates with you.

"Pursue love, and desire spiritual gifts, but especially that you may prophesy" (1 Corinthians 14:1). This Scripture comes right after the chapter about love in 1 Corinthians 13. If we do not clothe the gifts in love, we can wound people. Prophecy doesn't come from a person's own understanding (2 Peter 1:20). Supernatural knowledge delivered without wisdom and love can do more damage than good. I am thankful for every piece of training I have had in prophetic ministry. I have greatly benefitted from all of it. Revelation 19:10 sums it up beautifully, "For the essence of prophecy is to give a clear witness for Jesus" (NLT). A prophetic word should draw someone closer to Jesus. Prophetic

---

10. Brown, Driver, Briggs, and Gesenius. "Hebrew Lexicon entry for *ra'ah*." The KJV Old Testament Hebrew Lexicon, accessed March 1, 2015, http://www.biblestudytools.com/lexicons/hebrew/kjv/raah.html.
11. Ibid, "Hebrew Lexicon entry for *nabiy'*." The KJV Old Testament Hebrew Lexicon, accessed March 1, 2015, http://www.biblestudytools.com/lexicons/hebrew/kjv/nabiy.html.

evangelism can be a great witnessing tool. This is when Christians who want to do outreach ministry gather and pray. The Holy Spirit gives them words or pictures about what He wants them to do or where He wants them to go, as they go out and minister on the street in groups of two or three. This can have great impact on those who receive ministry. It is powerful when they hear that God sent someone to them with a specific word or prayer for healing. This is one way God reveals that He loves people and has a plan for their lives.

Paul told Timothy to not neglect the gift of prophecy he received when the elders laid hands on him (1 Timothy 4:14). We can have a spiritual gift from birth and be trained in it later in life. We can also receive it by the laying on of hands. God can give it to us anytime He desires. To receive training also helps one grow and gives opportunity to practice hearing God's voice. I have been blessed by prophetic words that I have received in training situations. God speaks and people are blessed.

First Corinthians 14:3 frames the boundaries for New Testament prophecy: "But one who prophesies strengthens others, encourages them, and comforts them" (NLT). These are healthy guidelines for prophetic words. Stick to encouragement, strengthening, and comfort. If you receive a warning, pray for protection and blessing for the person, but leave the warnings to those who are mature in prophetic ministry or called to the office of prophet. A warning can cause fear or condemnation if it is not delivered correctly. If it bothers you a lot, submit the word to a prophetic leader in your church. The Bible tells us to test the spirits to know if they are from God (1 John 4:1). In Bible school our sons were encouraged to continuously study the Bible for themselves and to inquire of God whether what they were being taught was the truth. God's truth will prevail.

God often speaks to me through pictures or visions. I will see a picture in my mind as I wait on Him or pray, and He will reveal the meaning of it. In 1989 I asked a traveling speaker advice about raising children. Our oldest child was two at the time. I could see that she was asking God what she should say and then she replied, "Don't let your kids watch anything about witchcraft or have any witchcraft articles or books in your house."

I was very surprised. I looked through our house and found a book about fairy tales and threw that out. As the years went by and I saw what was on television, I knew God had prepared me for the onslaught of evil coming even through children's media. I have noticed that God often speaks to me through visions, and when I watch anything that has a different source from God, knowing how God feels about evil and that He hates witchcraft, I open myself to see demonic visions. To see and hear clearly from God I have to watch what I see and hear. David wrote that he did not set anything base before his eyes (Psalm 101:3). This guards my mind from evil.

Discerning of Spirits

How did Jesus know when a demonic spirit was tormenting a person? He walked in the gift of discernment. He knew when the sickness or problem was the result of demonic oppression and when the person just needed healing: "That evening many demon-possessed people were brought to Jesus. He cast out the evil spirits with a simple command, and he healed all the sick" (Matthew 8:16). People traveled with Jesus; Luke 8 describes them this way: "And the twelve were with Him, and certain women who had been healed of evil spirits and infirmities—Mary called Magdalene, out of whom had come seven demons" (Luke 8:1-2). Jesus and His disciples went to a region called the Gadarenes. On the way two demon-possessed men who were so violent nobody could come near them met Jesus. The demons screamed at Jesus, "Why are you interfering with us, Son of God? Have you come here to torture us before God's appointed time?" (Matthew 8:29 NLT). There was a herd of pigs nearby and they begged Jesus to send them into the herd of pigs. Jesus gave the command and they left the men and entered the herd of pigs, which caused the pigs to run off a cliff and be drowned in the ocean. This was too much for the people of that town; they asked Jesus to leave (Matthew 8:28-34).

We don't have to be afraid of demons, but we should not be foolish and tread on ground where they have legal right to come. Occult and witchcraft activities open doors for demonic harassment. God hates witchcraft: "There shall not be found among you anyone who makes his son or his daughter pass through the fire, or one who practices witchcraft, or a soothsayer, or one who interprets omens, or a sorcerer, or one who conjures spells, or a medium, or a spiritist, or one who calls up the dead. For all who do these things are an abomination to the Lord, and because of these abominations the Lord your God drives them out from before you. You shall be blameless before the Lord your God" (Deuteronomy 18:10-13). Why is God so vehemently against this? He told the Israelites not to have any gods besides Him (Exodus 20:3). All of these practices use the power of demonic spirits to operate. God wants us to trust in Him and in the power of the Holy Spirit.

God is jealous for our love. He wants to have relationship with us. He doesn't want us to engage in any way with demonic activities, because He knows they will cause bondage. Satan doesn't give his power away for free. At first it may seem like that, but soon people will find themselves in a world governed by fear and control. The kingdom of God is about love. Christians are free to follow the Holy Spirit and love God. There is no greater joy than to live in the accepting love of our heavenly Father, "Long ago, even before he made the world, God chose us to be his very own through what Christ would do for us; he decided then to make us holy in his eyes, without a single fault—we who stand before him covered with his love" (Ephesians 1:4 TLB). We do not need any other power than God's power to walk in supernatural power. Jesus walked in the power of the Holy Spirit. We can follow His example.

People who walk strongly in the gift of discernment are very valuable in intercessory prayer, in healing ministry, or in deliverance ministry. They can often discern what kind of demonic spirit is operating in a person's life. If they don't know what the specific spirit is, they can at least tell whether a demonic spirit is at work or not. The gift can operate in different ways. The years that I was very involved with intercession for specific ministries, I had dreams in which the Holy Spirit revealed strategy about particular situations and gave me direction about how to pray. As I was pursuing God, the Holy Spirit would sometimes just bring revelation about a situation that I had been praying and thinking about. From time to time I received warnings about what the enemy was planning, and I could pray that it would not happen.

God connected me in such a way that I was in a position to communicate with one of the pastors if needed. It is crucial to be connected in relationship and in submission to church leadership for this gift to work best. Most pastors don't pay attention to a stranger coming to them and telling them things about their church. There needs to be a cohesive relationship. Once I shared something, I learned to leave it in the hands of the pastor or leader I gave it to. I can pray about it and for them, but what they do with the word is up to them. It is easy to feel rejected or not valued if a leader does not agree with the things you share. If there is value in what was shared, God will confirm it in another way. We are just messengers.

I make it a practice to pray back to God everything I receive from the Holy Spirit. Discernment of spirits is not only used to identify evil. It is also used to release good. As the Lord gives me His words and I pray them back, I am, in effect, releasing His will into the earth. I am discerning His will and agreeing with it in prayer. This is a very powerful ministry. I believe most of what I receive is for the purpose of prayer.

Tongues and Interpretation of Tongues

> "To another different kinds of tongues, to another the interpretation of tongues" (1 Corinthians 12:10).

When I realized that the Holy Spirit was my Friend, Guide, Helper, as well as my constant companion, I felt like I needed to come to know Him more. As I went to different Christian events in our region, and I saw that in some churches the people sometimes spoke or sang in tongues. This intrigued me. I went to the Christian bookstore and found two books on it. It was fascinating and I became convinced that I needed what they called the baptism of the Holy Spirit. John the Baptist said he baptized people with water but Jesus will, "baptize you with the Holy Spirit and fire" (Matthew 3:11).

The disciples experienced an outpouring of the Holy Spirit that caused quite a commotion in Jerusalem. While they were in the upper room, a sound came like a mighty wind and what looked like tongues of fire settle on them. They were all filled with the Holy Spirit and started to speak in different tongues as given by the Holy Spirit. A crowd gathered to find out what happened. The disciples appeared to be drunk, but people were astonished that they heard the message of Jesus in their native tongue. Three thousand people came to faith in Jesus that day.

In Acts 4 we find the believers gathered together, singing, and then they prayed, "And now, O Lord, hear their threats, and give us, your servants, great boldness in preaching your word. Stretch out your hand with healing power; may miraculous signs and wonders be done through the name of your holy servant Jesus. After this prayer, the meeting place shook, and they were all filled with the Holy Spirit. Then they preached the word of God with boldness" (Acts 4:29-31 NLT). Twice in the first four chapters of Acts we see the disciples receive a powerful infilling of the Holy Spirit. This resulted in many people coming to Jesus, as well as healings and deliverance from evil spirits (Acts 5:14-16).

In the following chapters in Acts, the religious leaders became jealous of the apostles' ministry and had them put in jail. An angel came during the night and opened the prison doors. The Holy Spirit told them to go and preach in the temple. They obeyed. You can imagine the consternation. The temple guards brought the apostles before the religious leaders and the high priest confronted them, telling them they were told not to speak in Jesus' name. The apostles replied they had to obey God rather than man (Acts 5:12-29). In Acts 5:32 we find a key to walking with the Holy Spirit. The apostles said, "We are witnesses of these things and so is the Holy Spirit, who is given by God to those who obey him" (NLT).

This doesn't mean that if we miss it, the Holy Spirit is mad at us and leaves us. It means if I don't obey His voice, I feel a grieving inside and I know that I let Him down. If I continue to not obey the Holy Spirit, He speaks less and less. When I ask forgiveness and set my heart on obeying God, I continue in walking with the Holy Spirit. Obedience is the key. There might be times that I am obedient and He is not speaking a whole lot. In that case, I just continue on the journey. I know He will speak to me when I need to hear His voice.

Discovering the Holy Spirit

When Jesus appeared to His disciples after His resurrection, He told the disciples as God sent Him, He sends them. He breathed on them and told them to receive the Holy Spirit (John 20:21-22). Then in Acts 2 and 4 the disciples received an infilling of the Holy Spirit. These powerful infillings gave them power for ministry and boldness to preach. When Peter went to Cornelius' house, the Holy Spirit fell on the Roman believers gathered there. In Corinth, Paul met some believers and he asked them which baptism they had received and they replied, John's baptism. Paul told them they should be baptized in the name of Jesus. After they were baptized, Paul laid hands on them and they received the Holy Spirit and started to speak in tongues (Acts 19:1-6).

In Acts 8 when the apostles heard that people in Samaria were baptized because they believed in Jesus, they sent Peter and John to them so that they might receive the Holy Spirit. This can be a bit confusing when you read it in the Bible, because don't we receive the Holy Spirit when we receive Jesus as our Savior? Salvation is when we come to believe in Jesus and baptism is a public confession of faith. The disciples laid hands on people and prayed for people to receive the Holy Spirit after they were saved and baptized. I think we can receive an infilling of the Holy Spirit more than once. I often ask the Holy Spirit to come and fill me. I need more of Jesus every day. I need more of the Holy Spirit daily. There were times in my life when those infillings was more visible. People prayed for me and my body shook or trembled. At other times it didn't feel like anything happened, but I see the Holy Spirit at work in my life. He is in us and with us, whether in His quiet tender presence or whether He comes in power and fire as in times of revival.

I see four different ways the disciples received the Holy Spirit:
- Jesus breathed on the disciples (John 20:21-22).
- Supernatural visitation: The Holy Spirit came with a supernatural visitation to the disciples in the upper room. He came upon the believers in Cornelius' house (Acts 10:44).
- Laying on of hands: The Holy Spirit was imparted through the laying on of hands. Peter and John, who were with the group

in the upper room where the Holy Spirit manifested, prayed for others to receive the Holy Spirit (Acts 8:14-17; 1 Timothy 4:14).

- Ask: The Bible tells us that God is a good Father and if we ask God for the Holy Spirit, He will give us the Holy Spirit (Luke 11:10-13).

In 1989 when I began to learn about the Holy Spirit I had a desire to receive more of Him in my life. I had a relationship with Jesus and I had heard of the Holy Spirit, but I was hungry for more. I started to read books about the Holy Spirit. One evening at our church service, there was an invitation to receive prayer and I went forward. As the pastor's wife prayed for me, she asked me if anyone had prayed for me to receive the Holy Spirit. I answered, "No," and she prayed for me to receive Holy Spirit. I felt the presence of God as she prayed for me, but nothing notable happened.

Some months went by and I still desired to receive the gift of speaking in tongues. I was like that persistent widow in Luke 18:1-7. One day as I was asking again, I heard one word and started to say it in faith, then another word came and after a while my prayer language started to flow. "For if I pray in a tongue, my spirit prays, but my understanding is unfruitful" (1 Corinthians 14:14). I speak out the words, but my mind doesn't understand them. It stirs my spirit. Who knows better what to pray than the Holy Spirit?

Once I read about a pastor who felt very unsettled one evening. He went into his office and prayed for a long time in the Spirit until he had peace. On his way to bed he passed his daughter's bedroom and for no particular reason that he could understand, he told her to take his car the next day. She did and was in an accident. She would have been killed if she had been driving her own car. Paul said he prayed with his spirit and he prayed with his understanding (1 Corinthians 14:15). Praying in the Spirit can also mean to engage, to set ourselves to hear and communicate with the Holy Spirit, leaning into Him to hear what to pray. A time of worship helps to set our focus on God. Sometimes my tears are prayers. The Holy Spirit alerts us when it is time to pray. If you are worried or concerned or have an unsettled feeling in your spirit, go and pray.

I have a cousin who shared with me that her kids were driving overnight to come and visit. She had a strong sense to pray for them that night. Early that morning they received a call that the trailer behind the car overturned and the car flipped over. It was a miracle that no one was hurt. Once again lives were saved because of prayer. Whether we pray in tongues or whether we pray with our understanding, it has an effect. God listens and He works.

Several of my friends had an immediate release of speaking in tongues when they were prayed for. A pastor's friend who grew up in a very traditional denomination dedicated his life to Jesus when he was in college. He had an unforgettable experience when he was filled with the Holy Spirit. He wept and his body trembled. This tall college student had an emotional meltdown when the Holy Spirit came upon him. It changed his life and he is a pastor today.

Recently I heard a friend's testimony. She received Jesus as a child. When she was fifteen she read about being filled with the Holy Spirit. The book led her through a prayer, repenting of sins. As she prayed for an infilling of the Holy Spirit, she was filled right there in her bedroom. Another friend shared that she didn't receive a prayer language when they prayed for her, but the Holy Spirit led her to repent of some occult games she had been involved in at college. Then she received an infilling of the Holy Spirit. When we pour water in a glass, we make sure the glass is clean. It is wise to ask the Holy Spirit if there is anything He wants you to repent from before you ask Him to fill you. Today I understand that the Holy Spirit fills us when we ask—whether a person starts to speak in tongues or not. I know powerfully anointed Christians who do not speak in tongues. Obedience is the key to hearing the Holy Spirit.

In Acts 8 Simon the sorcerer desired the gift of the Holy Spirit. He offered Peter and John money to receive the power of the Holy Spirit. He wanted to lay hands on people so that they would receive the Holy Spirit. Peter told him this gift cannot be bought with money: "You can have no part in this, for your heart is not right with God. Repent of your wickedness and pray to the Lord. Perhaps he will forgive your evil thoughts, for I can see that you are full of bitter jealousy and are held captive by sin" (Acts 8:21-23 NLT). Jesus went to the cross so we could be forgiven of our sins and our hearts could be cleaned. We simply need to ask with a sincere heart and He forgives us.

"Do not neglect the gift that is in you, which was given to you by prophecy with the laying on of the hands of the eldership" (1 Titus 4:14). When people pray for the infilling of the Holy Spirit, that person could receive the gifts of tongues too. Paul said, "I thank my God I speak with tongues more than you all" (1 Corinthians 14:18). He spoke in the language people could understand when he spoke in a church. If a person gives a word in tongues, there should be someone who can interpret it (1 Corinthians 14:6-12).

Praying in tongues strengthens us. It is a personal gift, unlike prophecy which strengthens the church (1 Corinthians 14:4). It comes from our spirit, but God uses our mouth and vocal cords to say the words. "For if I pray in tongues, my spirit is praying, but I don't understand what I am saying" (1 Corinthians 14:14 NLT). Praying in tongues has been very valuable to me in my personal prayer life. When I do not know what to pray, I pray in tongues until I receive direction from the Holy Spirit as to how to pray in English: "Pray all the time. Ask God for anything in line with the Holy Spirit's wishes. Plead with him, reminding him of your needs, and keep praying earnestly for all Christians everywhere" (Ephesians 6:18 TLB). The New King James reads "praying always with all prayer and supplication in the Spirit. Pray the blessing of God upon all His believers." The longer I live the Christian life, the more I see the importance of prayer and how God works through it. A friend gave my sons a word. Then he looked at me and said, "God is accelerating your children's destiny because you and your husband are praying." Praying is what a parent does for their children, but this encouraged me that yes, our prayers do have an effect.

Obedience in following the Holy Spirit is what is most important in the Holy Spirit's involvement in our lives. Being sensitive and obedient to the soft tender promptings of the Holy Spirit marks a Spirit-filled life. The gift of tongues won't help much if a person does not obey and follow the Holy Spirit. The Holy Spirit will not lead us to do things that disobey Scripture. He will lead us into the fruit of the Spirit—love, joy, peace, long-suffering, kindness, goodness, faithfulness, and self-control.

We don't have to know which gift or manifestation of the Spirit is working through us. I have operated at different times in many gifts without thinking whether it was a word of knowledge or discernment or something else. We simply need to develop a relationship with the Holy Spirit. He will bring the right word at the right time. He knows exactly what we need and how He wants to use us.

I often say, "Holy Spirit, wash me, Holy Spirit, fill me." Some years ago I saw a vision of a broken clay pot. I knew that broken pot represented my life. I watched as God poured oil on that pot and the pieces came together. The light of His presence shone through the cracks. It was His presence that was holding together those broken pieces. Through the years the Holy Spirit has taken the broken pieces in my life and restored my broken vessel. As I walk through life, the life and presence of God is being released through this clay pot (2 Corinthians 4:7). Even though the Holy Spirit doesn't leave me, my flesh can become overpowering when I don't spend time with Jesus. Then the Holy Spirit becomes more like a dim light on the inside. I prefer to take time to make room for Him. I need more of Him and less of me. I need Jesus to shine through me.

The Holy Spirit is like precious, fresh water. Jesus said, "'Anyone who believes in me may come and drink! For the Scriptures declare, "Rivers of living water will flow from his heart."' (When he said 'living water,' he was speaking of the Spirit, who would be given to everyone believing in him)" (John 7:37-38 NLT). It is just like the picture of light shining through the clay pot. We are clay pots holding His precious living water, the presence of the Holy Spirit. When we give someone a word of encouragement or pray for a person, we give them a refreshing drink of water.

> "And yet, O Lord, you are our Father. We are the clay, and you are the potter. We all are formed by your hand" (Isaiah 64:8 NLT).

Discussion Questions: Can I Receive the Gifts of the Spirit?

1. Read 1 Corinthians 1:14:3: "But he who prophesies speaks edification and exhortation and comfort to men." Discuss what you would do in the following scenarios:
   - You receive a negative word for the person you are praying for.
   - You do not get any word at all.
   - You get a word about sin in a person's life.

2. How do you unpack a picture that God gives you for a person? Discuss how to go from receiving the picture to sharing its interpretation.
   - Picture
   - Interpretation
   - Application

Discovering the Holy Spirit

3. Discuss what to do if you don't get an interpretation. (Do not make up an interpretation.)

_____

_____

_____

_____

4. Jesus did only what He saw His Father doing. The temptation in giving a prophetic word is to say more than what God is saying. Think about your personality. Are you a person of few words or one who uses many words? Keep that in mind when you share a word. What would be the biggest challenge for you in sharing a word?

_____

_____

_____

_____

5. If you do not get any word or picture over someone when you are praying for them, pray a blessing over the person. Look up Numbers 6:24-26. Write down areas of a person's life that you can bless.

_____

_____

_____

_____

6. A prophetic word can release a person into their destiny or a new area God has for them. If the group feels comfortable with it, ask for a volunteer to sit in the middle and then the others ask the Holy Spirit for an encouraging word or picture for that person. Or read 1 Corinthians 14:1-5 and choose a phrase or verse to focus on and ask the Holy Spirit to speak to you about it.

Chapter 9: How Do I Walk in the Fruit of the Spirit?

"Abide in Me, and I in you. As the branch cannot bear fruit of itself, unless it abides in the vine, neither can you, unless you abide in Me" (John 15:4)

How would you feel if a pastor and teacher, whose friendship you greatly valued and respected, told you that he was moving to a different city? It would be a big loss, because you greatly value his presence, friendship, and wisdom in your life. If he moved to another city though, you could still stay connected or visit each other once in a while. But if such a friend passed away, the loss would be huge. The disciples spent three years traveling with Jesus, learning from Him. They were with Him everywhere He went. They could not have imagined what was going to happen to their beloved Friend and Teacher.

When the time drew near that Jesus would be captured and crucified, He shared with His disciples that He would leave them soon. He told them that He was going to prepare a place for them. Thomas replied that they didn't know the road to where He was going, but Jesus was referring to a spiritual place. Once again Jesus gave them a spiritual answer, "I am the way, the truth, and the life. No one comes to the Father except through me" (John 14:6). The disciples often asked Jesus to explain to them what He meant in His parables. During His last days with His disciples, Jesus told them that He would not leave them like orphans, but He would ask the Father to send them a Helper who would be with them always, who would abide with them and live in them forever (John 14:16). Just as the loss of a friend or spiritual mentor would be a huge shock, you can imagine the shock Jesus' disciples must have experienced when Jesus died on the cross. It took them a while to comprehend what Jesus meant when He said He would send them the Helper, the Holy Spirit. They followed Jesus' instructions and waited for the Holy Spirit to come—this Helper who would replace their Teacher and beloved Friend's presence in their lives.

After the Holy Spirit was poured out, He had an important place in their walk with God. They asked new believers, "Did you receive the Holy Spirit when you believed?" (Acts 19:2), and they followed and obeyed the directions of the Holy Spirit. What a wonderful privilege that we also live in days when we can trust and follow the Holy Spirit for direction for our lives and to help us be the hands, feet, and voice of Jesus to those who need Him today.

The Bible calls our bodies the "temple" of the Holy Spirit: "Or do you not know that your body is the temple of the Holy Spirit who is in you, whom you have from God, and you are not your own?" (1 Corinthians 6:19). When we surrender our lives to Jesus, we lay down our own plans and decide to follow Jesus. We abdicate the throne of self and allow the Holy Spirit to come and lead and guide us. People like to play the game "King of the Hill." Most people like to be in control. They want to control their destiny, their life, and some even want to control other people. The Holy Spirit doesn't enter our lives to control us. He asks that we daily, willingly surrender. It is a humble attitude of *not my will, but Your will, God, because You know best.*

There are seasons when I know what God wants me to do and I simply continue with what He has put before me. At other times I feel a sense of unsettledness, and situations change. Those are more challenging times. Most people do not like change. Life is constantly changing. When I was in high school, we didn't have computers. Now it is unthinkable not to have a computer. Life has changed so much in the last thirty years. During times of change, I seek God and keep my heart open to hear Him. It is at these times that I must be careful not to follow my preconceived ideas, but ask God what I need to know. His plan usually unfolds over a period of time. A prophet once told me that transition takes three years. I have experienced it in my own life that going from one season to another takes time. As I obey one step at a time, the Holy Spirit unfolds God's plan.

There have been times when I set my mind on a direction and circumstances changed, or it just didn't work out the way that I thought it should. The Holy Spirit brought a change of direction. The first suggestion about change might come through a dream. Once I had a dream where I turned left at a specific traffic light. I didn't know the street name, but I drove past that intersection often. Next time I passed it I looked at the street names; it was Lighthouse Lane on the right, and Homeward Drive to the left. In the dream, I had turned left. I was wondering if God was saying I would be home more in the future. I had no intention of being at home more, but it was the right thing because God wanted me to write. It took me a while to figure out that it was actually God speaking to me because my mind was set on other things. They were even good things, but they were not God's plan. Prayer and a willingness to submit is the key. I can see why God tells us to become like little children because His kingdom works opposite to the world. In His kingdom, we humble ourselves and we submit to God's will; we follow and obey the Holy Spirit.

Another example of this was when I considered doing an internship at our city house of prayer. I really wanted to do it, but felt like the time commitment would be too much. I put it before the Lord and told God if He wanted me to do this, He would have to show me. Within a week the Holy Spirit came and changed my mind and showed me how I could fit it into my schedule. My husband supported the decision and the way opened up. I am thankful that I was willing to ask God what He wanted. It turned out to be a very blessed time, and I have a continued involvement with the house of prayer.

We need the Holy Spirit to bring forth the fruit of the Spirit. "So I say, let the Holy Spirit guide your lives. Then you won't be doing what your sinful nature craves. The sinful nature wants to do evil, which is just the opposite of what the Spirit wants" (Galatians 5:16-17 NLT). We need to know that our natural mind doesn't think good thoughts; that is why we need to learn to bring our thoughts and our desires under the submission of Jesus every day. "When you follow the desires of your sinful nature, the results are very clear: sexual immorality, impurity, lustful pleasures, idolatry, sorcery, hostility, quarreling, jealousy, outbursts of anger, selfish ambition, dissension, division, envy, drunkenness, wild parties, and other sins like these" (Galatians 5:19-21 NLT). Compare this to what the Holy Spirit brings forth in our lives: "But the Holy Spirit produces this kind of fruit in our lives: love, joy, peace, patience, kindness, goodness, faithfulness, gentleness, and self-control" (Galatians 5:22-23 NLT). If there is an area where I continuously see bad fruit, I ask the Holy Spirit to show me what is at the root of it. Some of the relationship problems between my husband and I were rooted in my judgments against my dad. The Holy Spirit revealed it to me through training seminars, books, people who prayed with me, and challenging situations that continued to come up that caused me to seek God for answers. It made a big difference to my life and in my family.

"No" is a very good word to know and use in the area of sin. If you have already decided not to do something, you will be less likely to sin. If you're still entertaining sin, it will be harder to say no: "Temptation comes from our own desires, which entice us and drag us into sin. These desires give birth to sinful actions. And when sin is allowed to grow, it gives birth to death" (James 1:14-15 NLT). I needed emotional healing and truth in many areas of my life. During this whole process the Holy Spirit was and still is very gentle with me. I have gone through times when the Holy Spirit put His foot down and told me not do something again. But even then I did not feel condemned. Instead I felt the reverential fear of the Lord and awe of God. He actually cares so much for me that He warns me about things that will bear bad fruit in me. He is aware of the consequences and I can trust Him to guide me as I listen and obey.

When I invited Jesus into my heart, my life didn't change radically. Because I grew up in a Christian home, I knew how to live a good life. I heard a testimony of a man who was instantly delivered of drugs and pornography addiction when he was saved. He became a pastor and because he was so performance-driven and had experienced a lot of rejection that it affected his family. His wife struggled with depression and he had a bad relationship with his children. It took time for God to heal those wounds. The issues of rejection, abandonment, performance, and other things like that are all part of the healing process of walking with the Holy Spirit. God also sent a missionary couple to this man and they mentored him. We have lived as we have so long, we are often not even aware of the areas in which our lives are dysfunctional. We are stuck in a rut until the Holy Spirit or a situation reveals the problems.

A man once testified that he had a normal childhood. But as he continued to share, he remembered that his dad had punched him in the nose and he remembered blood dripping on his shoes. He had grown up with physical abuse; this was his "normal." Patterns of abuse often repeat from generation to generation. We need the Holy Spirit to come and shine His light and bring us into freedom and greater health—spiritually, emotionally, relationally, and physically.

I believe the Holy Spirit is going to do mass deliverances and healings again. We don't have the time to do all the one-on-one counseling and deliverance that is needed. Many people need help. Follow and love Jesus. Whether He instantly delivers you or you need to get counseling, Jesus came to set the captives free, to break bondages, to heal wounds, and relieve emotional pain. We are on a journey in life, and we need to trust Him in the journey. There are times when we experience the "suddenlies" of God and times where He suddenly breaks through and brings a change in perspective. We can compare it to receiving an upgrade. It is a sudden thrust forward and a quicker change than what we normally expect. This is what happens when the Holy Spirit breaks in and brings revelation about a situation. When we know what is wrong, we can pray or change and adjust accordingly and be set free.

Jesus came to heal the brokenhearted, to set spiritual captives free, and bring joy to our sadness. He not only came to save us from our sins, but to make us whole. The first time the word *salvation* is used in the Bible is in Genesis 49:18, "I have waited for your salvation, O Lord!" The word used here is the Hebrew word *Yeshua;* it means salvation, deliverance, welfare, health, and prosperity.[12] "Beloved, I pray that you may prosper in all things and be in health, just as your soul prospers" (3 John 1:2). Financial prosperity does not necessarily cause our souls to prosper; it can easily be a stumbling block when it turns into the love of money (1 Timothy 6:10). When money is used the right way, it can

---

12. Brown, Driver, Briggs, and Gesenius. "Hebrew Lexicon entry for *Yeshuw'ah*." The KJV Old Testament Hebrew Lexicon, accessed March 1, 2015, http://www.biblestudytools.com/lexicons/hebrew/kjv/yeshuwah.html.

Discovering the Holy Spirit

bless and help people. God wants us to prosper body, soul, and spirit. In my fifties I had to refocus the way I ate because my body started to give me warning signs. If I didn't make changes, I was going to have engine trouble. I have learned to go to the Holy Spirit with the hurts in my soul and allow Him to bring healing. Through the years I learned to turn my spirit to God and meet with Him in that personal, intimate place to hear His voice and follow Him.

My husband comes from a very stable family. He grew up on a farm in South Africa. The farm was thirty miles out of town and the kids had to go to a boarding school. When we both went through prayer ministry training, the Holy Spirit took him back to his boarding school years to bring healing in some areas. He remembered how he dreaded to go back to boarding school at the end of the weekend. He saw himself as a little boy going up the stairs of the boarding school, crying. He felt abandoned even though it wasn't his parents' fault. As he received prayer, he saw Jesus waiting for him at the stairs, taking his hand, and walking into the boarding school with him. He had a hurt in his heart because he didn't have a parent to read him a story or tuck him in at night. During the prayer time, he saw himself as a young boy in the dorm; Jesus was sitting on the side of his bed, reading a story to him. That brought great comfort and healing to his heart.

When our middle son was around eleven years old, he became so fearful at night that he couldn't fall asleep. I prayed for him and took authority over a spirit of fear and commanded it to go, but it didn't help. One day I remembered that his tonsils had been removed when he was two years old. He was very afraid in the evenings after that. When I prayed with him about it, he remembered that his dad wasn't allowed in the operating room and he felt all alone when a nurse pushed him into the room. He felt like there was nobody there to help him. I prayed and asked Jesus what He wanted my son to know about this situation. He saw that Jesus was walking with him as he was pushed into the operating room. That comforted him greatly. He told me that he often felt like someone was going to grab him when he walked into the bathroom or our unfinished basement. As we prayed, the Holy Spirit showed him he had been kicking and screaming when they wanted to give him the anesthesia and the nurses had to hold him down on the table. Going to the unfinished basement or the bathroom triggered a similar feeling as he had then, and made him feel like someone was going to grab him. When the Holy Spirit showed him the connection, the truth set him free and he didn't have those feelings anymore.

If a reaction is rooted in a traumatic incident from childhood, a person may have difficulty getting rid of the negative feelings that get triggered again and again. The problem is that the feelings emerge and the incident does not. Additionally, every situation that vaguely resembles that situation can trigger the feelings. This only makes it more challenging to find the root cause of the behaviors. I have learned to pray and press in when situations like this come up. I press in until the Holy Spirit reveals what is going on. Why is this child struggling in this area of his life? When the specific belief is revealed, for example, "I felt all alone," then I prayed with the child and asked Jesus what He wanted to reveal to the child about the situation. If there was trauma involved, I also pray that the Holy Spirit will cleanse that time when the incident happened.

This is why Jesus died, to set the captives free. Jesus said, "And you shall know the truth, and the truth shall make you free" (John 8:32). When my son knew the truth that Jesus was with him, it uprooted the fear he felt and he wasn't afraid anymore. Only a revelation from the Holy Spirit, God, or Jesus can do that. I could tell him that Jesus was with him all the time, but it wouldn't have the same effect as when Jesus personally revealed it to him. Often when there is consistent bad fruit, there is a bad root. My son tried on the surface to overcome his fear. He tried to fall asleep. I prayed for him, again and again, but it didn't make much difference. I took authority over a spirit of fear, but it didn't help. It helped to find the root. We need God's discernment in every situation to show us the roots of problems. They can be demonic or rooted in a lie. Then we must pray accordingly. When there is a root involved, it is impossible to overcome on the surface. It is much better if Jesus cleanses the roots; then it is easier to produce good fruit. It comes from the inside and is genuine. It is not the result of self-effort and a desire to try and change behavior. If commanding a demonic spirit to go solves the problem, then command it to go! But not every problem is caused by a demonic spirit.

They say it takes twenty-one days to establish or change a habit. Some people manage to change by just breaking the habit for twenty-one days. A bad habit can progress and become an addiction. Pathways are formed in the brain that trigger that same pattern again and again. New pathways need to be formed in the brain. God can set a person free of an addiction in an instant and sometimes He does; other times it's a process. However He works in your life, help is available, so seek help if you need it.

A few years into our marriage I saw a vision of a man propped up with wooden poles. One by one these props were removed and finally the man fell back into the arms of Jesus. I realized this vision was what God was doing in my life. I had these props that kept me up. It felt safe when my husband got a pay check every month; I didn't have to trust God. Then we moved and my husband started with an engineering consultation business; the paycheck wasn't as regular every month. God used this to work in different areas of my life to reveal where I put my trust. He took my props away one by one. In the process, He brought me into a place of greater freedom in Him. My joy in Him is not dependent on how big my house is or how much money I have. He has brought me to a place where I find my joy is only in Him. Even when I go through a difficult time or disappointment, I have learned to run to Jesus.

In Luke 15 we find the Prodigal Son who remembered his father's house when he was out of money, had no food, and was taking care of the pigs. He went back to his father's house. This dad responded very differently than expected, and not the way many others have experienced: "So he returned home to his father. And while he was still a long way off, his father saw him coming. Filled with love and compassion, he ran to his son, embraced him, and kissed him" (Luke 15:20).

When you come to rest in the arms of a father who loves and accepts you, you will not run to any other place. It is the safest place in the whole world. The easiest way to enter into His presence is through worship. The words of the songs focus my attention on God. Whatever the problem is, run into His presence; turn your face to Him. You cannot mess up so badly that He can't or won't forgive you. He is the God of second chances. Sometimes a person needs to hit rock bottom, to be sick of sin. Sometimes life hurts a great deal before a person starts seeking God. Our heavenly Father is not surprised by this. He knows what will cause a person to turn.

When you have learned how to enter into His presence, there is no turning back. There is nothing like His comforting presence. There is no greater joy or peace than enjoying the presence of Almighty God. It reminds me of Psalm 45:11, "So the King will greatly desire your beauty; because He is your Lord, worship Him." It is amazing to think that God, the King of the Universe, desires a relationship with us. When we return that desire and desire to know Him, we find great joy and peace, a taste of eternity.

I have gone through seasons when I felt God's presence more and other seasons when it felt like He was far away. I walk by faith and not by how I felt. In Bible school our son said the leader shared with the group that he doesn't say, *God said,* more than two times a year, unless he is very sure, because we can miss it. One year a student told him God wanted him to go to ministry school, but the next year God told him to switch schools. He advised them to do what they felt God wanted them to do, but that they should not add the words, *God said,* because we make mistakes. When we put God's authority behind what we do, by saying, "God said" or "God told me," it can make those we speak to feel as though they can't challenge what *God said,* even if they disagree. It shuts the door to receive counsel. "Where there is no counsel, the people fall; but in the multitude of counselors there is safety" (Proverbs 11:14).

Jesus truly laid down all His desires. He had no home. He had no earthly possessions. He had one agenda and that was to do the will of His Father, and He accomplished His Father's will. It is a daily process to die to my desires and follow Jesus. "And those who are Christ's have crucified the flesh with its passions and desires" (Galatians 5:24). It doesn't mean that God will not sometimes come and give us something our heart desires; that is what a loving father does. Our desires should not be first in our hearts. Our love for Jesus should be in first place.

A father knows what is best for His children. One of the most valuable lessons that I am learning is to have joy and peace regardless of my circumstances. We cannot control our circumstances, and it is unrealistic to think we will never have a problem or walk through a trial. The opposite is true the bigger God's plan is for your life. When His plan is big, the training and testing to develop your character is fiercest. It is usually the difficulties and hardships that give us deep roots in God, "I pray that Christ will be more and more at home in your hearts, living within you as you trust in Him. May your roots go down deep into the soil of God's marvelous love, and may you be able to feel and understand, as all God's children should, how long, how wide, how deep, and how high his love really is, and to experience this love for yourselves" (Ephesians 3:17-19 TLB).

Jesus gave us a beautiful picture of a grapevine in John 15. He said He is the Vine and we are the branches. It is a beautiful revelation of an intimate relationship with Jesus: "Dwell in Me, and I will dwell in you. [Live in Me, and I will live in you.] Just as no branch can bear fruit of itself without abiding in (being vitally united to) the vine, neither can you bear fruit unless you abide in Me" (John 15:4 AMP). The words, "dwell in Me, live in Me" reveal a continuous ongoing relationship.

When I was in school, I read my devotional every evening and prayed, but during the day I forgot about God. When I gave my life to Jesus, I was still very performance oriented. As I learned and grew in my relationship with Him, it changed from a master/servant to father/child and then an intimate, best friend relationship. A preacher once said that we should turn our focus to God a couple of times a day and ask, *Holy Spirit, what are You doing today?* However we do it, if we continue to become more aware of God's involvement in our lives each day, we will be more aware of His Spirit too. When our children were young I often vacuumed and cleaned while I had a worship CD on. The words of the songs drew my mind to think about Jesus while I was doing relatively mindless tasks. "And now just as you trusted Christ to save you, trust him, too, for each day's problems, live in vital union with him. Let your roots grow down into him and draw up nourishment from him" (Colossians 2:6-7 TLB).

When our daughter was four and her brother two years old, they played house. They carried nearly all their toys to the living room and lined them up against the imaginary wall of their house; they played for two to three hours. My daughter always had her children's Bible in the lineup too; it was part of her life and even her playtime. We, as parents, can affect our children to love Jesus. Boys and girls have different challenges as they grow up. Girls struggle to find their identity in the midst of the media where beautiful models with perfect figures are presented as what's desirable. They can become very focused on outward beauty if they do not learn how God values them. Boys have different challenges. They love action and adventure and electronic games can draw them in and become like an addiction. My biggest struggle with our boys was to limit the amount of time they played games and get them to stick to it. At some point, our oldest son in sixth grade had trouble reading his Bible. The Holy Spirit revealed that a computer game he was playing was causing the problem. As he repented of participating in the game and things that God forbade people in the Bible to do, Jesus set him free. After that bad experience, he didn't play that game again.

Jesus told them His Father is the Gardener who prunes the grapes. In John 15:3 Jesus told the disciples that they are already been pruned by the messages He is sharing with them. When we learn the truth from the Bible and make good decisions it can save us much heartache. We are sanctified and cleansed by the washing of the Word (Ephesians 5:26). I want to learn from the Word and others' mistakes instead of continually making my own. God is a good Father; when He prunes our lives, it has purpose. His plan is that we will bear more fruit. A real grapevine is pruned back every year. If it is not pruned, it might have plenty of fruit the next year, but the fruit will not be of good quality. Pruning keeps the vine in balance, so it will consistently produce a good harvest. The vinedresser prunes the grapevine in such a way that he can get the best crop year after year. It is the same for us; any pruning we go through is so we will be fruitful to the best degree. It might not be comfortable at the time, but God sees the bigger picture. When we bring forth a bountiful harvest, we bring honor to God (John 15:8). God takes us through challenges, difficulties, and daily struggles with His greater purpose in mind.

I read an article of a lady journalist who decided to do an experiment. She was trying to keep the Ten Commandments and live like a Christian should for a week. She was not a Christian. She came to the conclusion that it was impossible. She found herself cursing at times and getting angry; the harder she tried, the worse it got. Her attempt to obey biblical principles wasn't a success. Obedience is smoother when it comes from the inside out. Jesus told the Pharisees that they cleaned the cups on the outside, but in their hearts they were full of greed and self-indulgence. If they cleaned the inside of the cup, the outside would be clean too. The same is true for us. If our hearts are pure, our motives and our actions will be pure too. John 15:16 is the goal God wants to accomplish in our lives—to bear lasting fruit or fruit that remains. "Whatever you ask the Father in My name He may give you" (John 15:16). Why will He give us this fruit? Because we will ask according to His desire, and not our own; and it will bring blessing and not harm.

The Holy Spirit brings forth the fruit of the Spirit in us when we walk with Him and abide in Him. Our flesh can act good, gentle, and kind, but the true fruit of the Spirit comes from allowing our spirits to be saturated with His presence. There have been times in my first years at the house of prayer when I spent hours with Jesus, reading my Bible, soaking in His presence, and praying. When I stopped at the store on my way home, I often noticed that people smiled at me. I wondered why and later realized I was walking around with a smile on my face. I was so filled to overflowing that I could not contain it on the inside. It flowed over and showed on my face. I can already hear you saying, "I don't have hours to spend with Jesus," and that is okay. Give Him the fifteen or thirty minutes or an hour that you have. I use the time when I am driving to pray or listen to Christian radio or a worship CD. Grab the opportunities that you can use to fill your spiritual tank.

The Holy Spirit is on a mission to change us to become more like Jesus and live a fruitful life, accomplishing the plans and purposes God has for us. One of my Bible study leaders used to say, "God is more interested in our character than our comfort." That wasn't exactly what I wanted to hear, but I learned that lesson well. When I came through a challenge, hardship, or difficulty, I grew spiritually in my relationship, faith, and trust in God. "In this you greatly rejoice, though now for a little while, if need be, you have been grieved by various trials, that the genuineness of your faith, being much more precious than gold that perishes, though it is tested by fire, may be found to praise, honor, and glory at the revelation of Jesus Christ" (1 Peter 1:6-7).

There have been times when it felt like I came to a dead end or an impossible next step. Looking back at what God has done in my life, I see how many impossible situations He got me through. I had faith that He would help me each time. One way to build faith is to hear the testimonies of other Christians. It encourages me to hear their stories. If God can do it for them, He will do it for me too. This is part of developing our personal history in God. No one has walked your exact path before, and no one else will. God has a unique plan for your life. Follow Him!

God reveals Himself as our Father. He wants us to fully trust Him, like a child trusts a parent. "I've (Jesus) loved you the way my Father has loved me. Make yourselves at home in my love" (John 15:9 MSG). Jesus loves us the same way His Father loves Him. Being a parent I know how much I love my children. Even now that they are grown up I try to keep updated about what is going on in their lives. I want to know if they have everything they need, and I help them as much as I can without hindering their independence as they move on in life. God is even more involved with our lives. His Holy Spirit lives in us, so He knows even before we tell Him how we are doing. Even though He knows everything, He wants us to live in relationship with Him and tell Him what is going on in our lives and our hearts. King David often poured out his heart to God. He told God how his enemies were pursuing him and then turned around and asked God to cleanse his heart. He ended his time of prayer by glorifying and praising God.

Jesus said that He did nothing in His own power. He revealed His connectedness to His Father: "Do you not believe that I am in the Father, and the Father in Me? The words that I speak to you I do not speak on My own authority; but the Father who dwells in Me does the works" (John 14:10). Jesus' life was an example for us of how to live and walk on earth abiding in God. We have the Holy Spirit who dwells in us and works through us. Guest speakers once visited our church. After the husband and wife spoke, we prayed for them. Even before we prayed, I felt like the Holy Spirit was showing me that I should pray Psalm 1 for them: "They are like trees along a river bank bearing luscious fruit each season without fail. Their leaves shall never wither, and all they do shall prosper" (Psalm 1:3 TLB).

God was saying that He wanted them to be like trees along a riverbank, drawing living water from the Holy Spirit to stand strong in Him, whether it was raining or the sun shone—no matter what the outward circumstances were. The wife shared that she had been memorizing Psalm 1 the past two weeks. I had no idea; the Holy Spirit knew. God confirmed to them that He knew exactly what was going on in their lives. It is the Holy Spirit who works through a human vessel. "We now have this light shining in our hearts, but we ourselves are like fragile clay jars containing this great treasure. This makes it clear that our great power is from God, not from ourselves" (2 Corinthians 4:7).

We see Jesus obey the will of His Father on earth even unto death. He didn't sometimes do things God's way and other times His own way. He completely trusted God that God knew best and that God's will was the best way. He took time to pray and draw near to His Father, even through the night at times. Jesus did not have stress or fear in His relationship with His dad. Yes, he was under extreme pressure praying in the garden, knowing what was going to happen, but He obeyed. Jesus knew there was much more in store than the hours of suffering. He saw eternity and those who would join Him in eternity; He could endure the suffering for the sake of the breakthrough it would bring. The sins of mankind would be forgiven, and those who chose to receive His sacrifice on the cross would be forgiven and spend eternity with Him. He knew the suffering had a greater purpose and God didn't love Him less.

The second part of John 15:9 reads, "Make yourselves at home in my love"; other translations read it as "remain, abide, or live in My love." There is nothing more wonderful than to walk and live in such a relationship with God, Jesus, and the Holy Spirit. When we have confessed all known sins, keep short accounts with God, repent quickly when we sin, and live in that place of His unsurpassing peace, no money or earthly treasures can take the place of God's joy (Philippians 4:7).

Hermie Reynolds

Discussion Questions: How Do I Walk in the Fruit of the Spirit?

1. Read Galatians 5:19-23. Make two columns: "Works of the Flesh" and "Fruit of the Spirit." Highlight/circle down the fruit of the Spirit that you need the Holy Spirit to help you with most.

2. Continuous bad fruit can be the result of a bad habit or an area in your character that needs to grow. Think about the area of the fruit of the Spirit that you circled in number one. Take a few minutes and ask the Holy Spirit to show you if there are any connections and what is the underlying issue of the struggle.

3. Read James 1:26 and Proverbs 25:11 and discuss what you learn about words from these verses. Give examples of words being a blessing or a curse in someone's life.

4. Focus on John 15:5-16. Pick a phrase or verse and ask the Holy Spirit to speak to you about it. Write down what He says.

_____
_____
_____
_____
_____
_____
_____
_____

Chapter 10: How Do I Hear the Holy Spirit?

> "The Lord says, 'I will guide you along the best pathway for your life. I will advise you and watch over you. Do not be like a senseless horse or mule that needs a bit and bridle to keep it under control'" (Psalm 32:8-9 NLT).

Since the day I learned God speaks to us, I have desired to hear His voice. The only problem was I didn't hear Him speak to me much. I did sometimes read a Scripture that stirred my heart and I wrote them down. There were also times when I prayed or waited in His presence at home or during worship at church or in group prayer times, and I saw a picture in my mind.

Pondering the picture I understood that God was speaking to me. I could understand some of what He was saying, but I still felt like there was more. But I wasn't sure what. It is similar to what the disciples experienced with the parables Jesus told. On the surface Jesus used language and pictures that the people were familiar with—a farmer, a king, sowing seed. But these parables explained to the people who God was and communicated spiritual truths. When they were alone, the disciples often asked Jesus to explain the parables.

As I was teaching an art class with a biblical theme once, I taught about the sower in Mark 4:14-20. The next week a boy told me he really liked the parable and asked if I could share it again. As I shared it again, he told me about a teenager who had a challenging relationship with her parents and didn't want to know anything about God. As we went through the different soils, the Holy Spirit showed me that we should pray for this friend, that her hardened heart would become like the good soil to receive the words of truth that people were sowing in her life, and that she will become receptive to hear about Jesus. In an instant I had received prayer strategy for this situation from this parable that I hadn't thought of before.

Sometimes when we receive a picture or a word, the revelation comes in layers. Layers unfold as different people share a vision or word with you and then the Holy Spirit uses it to speak to you. When God is speaking to me about a Scripture or a specific theme, I usually see other things that connect with it. After that art class, I was driving to pick up a friend's daughter from school and I saw a license plate: "ILUVCECE." That was the name of the girl that we had prayed for! Her friends called her Ce Ce. I realized Jesus was saying He loved this girl! He really cared about her!

As a young Christian I wanted God to speak to me more clearly in my everyday life. What I didn't realize was that I wanted God to give me orders. I wanted Him to say, *do this, do that*, but that's not what He wanted. He wanted to have a relationship with me. Through the years, I have grown in recognizing the ways God speaks. Learning to recognize His voice is like learning a foreign language. God speaks to us through the Bible, but also through words, pictures, impressions, dreams, other people, friends, and limitless ways. We have to be on the alert to get tuned in to what He is saying or it might just go past us without being noticed. God has given us a free will. If He just tells us what to do with our lives, then we have no choice to make and we just have to do it. If He speaks through symbolic language, dreams, pictures, or impressions, then we have the choice whether we want to search it out and find out if God is speaking to us or not. The clearer His instructions, the less choice we have. If the instructions aren't that clear, then there is more grace in the situation if we miss it or don't get it 100 percent right. God is focused on obedience coming from relationship. It is the same as when a parent wants a child to do the right thing, but wants them to make that choice themselves.

God spoke to Ananias in a vision and told him to go to Straight Street and pray for Saul. Ananias had heard that Saul persecuted Christians, and he was a bit hesitant about going. God told him Saul was His chosen vessel to take the message of Jesus to the Gentile nations. Ananias wasn't given much choice in this situation; this message was very clear. God needed someone who would be obedient and go to Saul. Ananias obeyed and went to pray for Saul (Acts 9:10-17). God could have supernaturally spoken to Paul and removed the blindness, but He asked Ananias to go and pray for Paul.

Early on I learned that there is a hard way I can learn spiritual lessons or there is an easier way. Jesus told His disciples in John 15 that He is the Vine and we are the branches. His Father is the Gardener who prunes the branches that do not bear fruit. He continues to tell them that they have already been pruned by listening to His teachings. When I read this, it felt that I was always learning lessons the hard way. I read Psalm 32:8-9 and asked God to teach me through His Word or through other people rather than learning everything by making mistakes. It is not that I don't make any mistakes, but since that time I began to learn more from other people, books, and messages that came across my path.

In John 10 Jesus told the parable of the sheep that follow the shepherd's voice. The shepherd knows his sheep. "They won't follow a stranger; they will run from him because they don't know his voice" (John 10:5 NLT). Just as a baby recognizes her mother and father's voice, we come to know our heavenly Father's voice. When we give our lives to Jesus, we step into this journey of walking, following, and obeying Him.

Adam and Eve had a relationship with God in the garden of Eden. When they sinned they hid from God. They heard God walking in the garden during the early evening. (Genesis 3:8). They had heard Him come before; they knew who He was. We were also created to have a relationship with God. Jesus is the door through which we enter into this relationship (John 10:7-9). It is not the end, but the beginning of a life in which we walk with God. We have a relationship with God here on earth. Through it, we get to know Him and learn how He speaks to us.

I love to walk on the beach or sit in a beautiful garden and spend time with God. Yet, I don't have a private garden at our current home. My heart and my spirit is the garden where I can meet Jesus every day. Song of Songs 4:12 reads, "You are my private garden, my treasure, my bride, a secluded spring, a hidden fountain" (NLT). A private garden would be for the enjoyment of the King only. That is the place the Holy

Discovering the Holy Spirit

Spirit is seeking, a place where we make room and time for Him. I have found that I treasure that time with Jesus. I have no agenda. I make a different time for spiritual disciplines—a specific time for praying for others, a time for reading and studying the Bible.

It is good to have time to just sit with Jesus and ask what is on His mind or what would He like to do. If I don't sense something specific, I just sit with Him. I sit still with my eyes closed, experiencing His peace and quiet presence. Other times He may bring a Scripture to my mind or take me through a journey in Scriptures. Maybe I will see a vision that will set me on a trail of searching out Scripture, seeking what He is saying to me. Ephesians 3:17 describes this life of living with the Holy Spirit beautifully: "May Christ through your faith [actually] dwell (settle down, abide, make His permanent home) in your hearts. May you be rooted deep in love and founded securely on love" (AMP).

It was a process to get to the place where I can walk and live from this place of rest. As a one-year-old child I was burned with boiling water. Much later in life I learned that this trauma had opened a door for fear to enter my life. I often felt fear about the future. When I learned more about who God was, the fear became less, but I still woke up at night and felt afraid about the future. It wasn't about anything specific; it was just a vague fear. Then I saw a vision about an airplane; its cargo door was wide open. As I prayed, the Lord showed me that there was a door to my life that was open and the enemy was using it to bring fearful thoughts. As I prayed and closed that door, the fear disappeared.

My background as a track and cross-country runner caused me to become very performance oriented, and that carried over into my spiritual life. Instead of resting and being at peace in God, I was focused on striving and trying to perform well. God had to heal the hurts, wounds, and wrong beliefs of my past to bring me to that place of rest and peace in Him. Today when a situation tries to pull me out of that place of being secure in my Father's love, I quickly run back to Him. He is my safe and secure place.

In his autobiography, Reinhard Bonnke writes, "A Divine Appointment: 'Which thread should I choose, Lord? There are so many. They hang before my eyes like strands of silk in a doorway. Each promising that it will weave the finest tapestry of my life. But it is not my tapestry. It is not my life. So again I ask, which thread do I choose? Which strand will pass through the eye of the needle?'"[13]

There were several times in my life when I came to such an intersection, asking which way I should choose. Often both ways looked like the right way. This was not easy. I learned to say, *I choose God's way and not my own way*, and then I would press into Him to show me the way. As I did this, it would unfold. Sometimes He spoke through a Scripture or a picture or a friend. When I am waiting for an answer, I keep my eyes open. The things I see, read, or just happen to cross my path by coincidence are often nudges from the Holy Spirit.

Fasting is also a way to hear from God. There are different ways to fast. You can fast from food, drinking only water; you can do a Daniel fast, eating mainly vegetables for twenty-one days. Our family has fasted from television for forty days more than once. It was surprising to see how the kids' prophetic gifts opened up and the amazing pictures they received from God when we did this. I have done word fasts when I was intentionally careful with my words and what I said. But the most important aspect of fasting is to set aside something you do, and use that time to seek God.

God speaks to us in many different ways. They include:

Scripture

It is very valuable to memorize Scripture. The Holy Spirit will use it. Often when I pray for someone, the Holy Spirit will bring a Scripture to my mind. I don't know them all by heart, but most of the time I know where to find it or know what it says. One time during a prayer class, we prayed for a young lady. I felt impressed to share the parable about the kingdom of heaven (Matthew 13:44-45). I told this young lady that she had already seen the value of the kingdom of God at a young age. Another lady shared the same passage and told her she was like a precious pearl to Jesus. Afterward the girl shared that God had spoken this parable to her both ways at a recent camp—that the

---
13. Bonnke, Reinhard, *Living a Life of Fire*, (Harvester Services, Inc., 2010), p. 9.

kingdom of God is a pearl and that she is a pearl too. This was a great confirmation to her.

The Holy Spirit uses what we know. He will use the Scriptures that you have read and memorized when you pray for people, or He will bring Scripture to remembrance when you need it. Some people enjoy reading the Bible chronologically chapter by chapter; others study a specific chapter or a theme. If you are studying the Bible for yourself, do what you enjoy and let the Holy Spirit lead you. When I read a Scripture and feel the Holy Spirit highlight it, I pause there for a while and ask, *What is God's purpose in highlighting this Scripture to me? Is He bringing truth to me? Is it a Scripture that I can turn into prayer? Does He want me to look up cross references or do further study?* The Holy Spirit already knows God's purpose in what we're reading and studying and how to lead us to receive the truth we need at that time.

One morning I was reading Song of Songs 2:16: "My beloved is mine, and I am his." For about an hour I couldn't get away from this verse, and the Holy Spirit just ministered the love of Jesus to my heart. When the Holy Spirit's focus is on a verse, just stay there. I ask, *Holy Spirit, come and speak to me about what I read.* Talk to God about what you read. Consider this verse, "casting all your care upon Him, for He cares for you" (1 Peter 5:7). Take some time to release your cares to Him. Make the Bible interactive. Ask the Holy Spirit questions and expect Him to lead you. You will receive more from reading with the involvement of the Holy Spirit.

Songs

God often uses songs to minister to me. Some mornings I wake up and there is a song in my spirit. Often it will just be a phrase or part of a song and I will have to go and look up the words because the message of what the Holy Spirit is speaking to me is in the song. One evening my husband said he had difficulty falling asleep. I asked him why. He said, "My spirit can't stop singing!" I asked him what song he was singing. He said it was a song about God's faithfulness. I smiled and thought that was a great problem to have. I sensed that his spirit and the Holy Spirit were rejoicing together about God's faithfulness.

Sometimes the Holy Spirit will highlight a phrase in a song. I try to write down the different things the Holy Spirit speaks to me, because when I look at the different parts of the puzzle I can see how it connects. One time I had a dream about sitting in a tent, singing a song about following Jesus. Thinking about the dream, I realized a tent is not a permanent dwelling. It meant that I don't have such rigid walls that it is difficult to move me when God wanted to move me. That is how I want to be—sensitive to the voice of the Holy Spirit and able to easily follow and obey Him as He leads.

Impressions

During the day, many random thoughts run through our minds. We have to discern whether they are just our own thoughts, those of the enemy, or the Holy Spirit's thoughts. When I think about a person, I pray for the person or I call when I feel that is what the Holy Spirit wants me to do. When I see someone in the street who looks like someone I know, I pray for the person whom I am reminded of.

The Holy Spirit will bring people to mind who need prayer. One day I thought of a family member who lived in another country. The next day I talked to them and there was a situation that needed prayer. The Holy Spirit knows about everything that is happening on earth. He knows who needs prayer. He knows who He can alert to pray for a need. He just needs someone to take that thought and turn it into prayer.

Most of the times I thought I should call a friend were from the Holy Spirit. He can give you the feeling you should take a different road to work. I read a testimony of a man who had to pick up a friend. He had to cross a big bridge, but as he approached it he saw a vision of the bridge collapsing and heard the Holy Spirit telling him to stop. He stopped right before the bridge, and it actually did collapse! He not only saved his own life, but also those who were following behind him. This is God's heart. He desires a people who can hear His voice and respond through prayer and action.

In times past I have felt the bad effects of another's bad attitude toward me. Once someone was jealous of me and I felt it. Even well-intended prayers that are from the soul realm or a person's own thoughts can work like witchcraft against the person who is being prayed for. We must pray God's thoughts and plans over people. During a season when I was misunderstood, I experienced hopelessness and depression, seemingly for no reason. I read a book that explained how people release demonic attack when they pray their own will on someone. I can understand why the Bible says, "Do all that you can to live in peace with everyone" (Romans 12:18). It releases warfare and demonic resistance against us when we don't live in peace with people.

One morning after a time of prayer I was driving home from the house of prayer. I turned on a road and they were busy directing traffic past the light to turn on the next light and redirect it back on that road. I turned where I usually turned, but that was not what I was supposed to do. Three lights later a man stopped next to me on his motorcycle, yelling at me because I made the wrong turn. I was so stunned I didn't say a word. Afterward I just felt awful, like "yuck." He had just dumped a lot of "yuck" on me in the spirit through his words. We can bless people or curse people with our words: "Death and life are in the power of the tongue, and those who love it will eat its fruit" (Proverbs 18:21). I asked the Holy Spirit to wash me of the effect of those words.

Riddles

A riddle or a dark saying is like the parables Jesus told. You have to search out the meaning. One time I shared a message about judgments and the life-changing impact repenting of those judgments had on my life. That night I had a dream that I took all the coins out of my wallet and gave most of them away. I realized that coins are "change"; the dream was about sharing how God changed my life. I had to look at the symbols and ask the Holy Spirit to bring revelation so I could understand it.

God hasn't spoken to me in an audible way. He mostly speaks to me through Scripture, visions, dreams, or just the sense of peace or urgency in my heart. When I feel I need to pray for someone I don't question whether it is the Holy Spirit. I just obey and take a few minutes to pray. When I don't have peace about a situation, I press in and ask God for answers. Sometimes the answer comes a day or two days later, but I press in until I get an answer or feel peace about the situation. The parable about the widow who kept asking the judge to give her justice is applicable here. At first the judge ignored her, but then he granted her request (Luke 18:3-7). When we continue to seek God about something, He sees that we are serious about getting an answer: "I love those who love me, and those who seek me early and diligently shall find me" (Proverbs 8:17 AMP).

The disciples asked Jesus why He spoke in parables (Matthew 13:10). Jesus answered that to those who listen, more will be given. Revelation from God is often hidden and these mysteries or treasures are available to those who seek them. The Scripture talks about not casting pearls before swine (Matthew 7:6). God gives more revelation to those who hunger and seek Him. When He speaks in riddles, those who do not desire to hear Him will not understand it. The life of a seed is hidden on the inside. It is not apparent from the outside. "Again, the kingdom of heaven is like treasure hidden in a field, which a man found and hid; and for joy over it he goes and sells all that he has and buys that field" (Matthew 13:44).

Dreams and Visions

God speaks to people through dreams in the Bible. God even speaks to people who don't know Him in dreams. Pharaoh had a dream and God gave Joseph the interpretation of the dream (Genesis 41:1-36). Joseph told Pharaoh that God showed the king what is going to take place. He explained the dream and then shared wisdom what to do about the dream. Daniel interpreted Nebuchadnezzar's dream. He told Nebuchadnezzar that God, who reveals secrets, showed the king what will happen in the future (Daniel 2:3-47). God spoke to Joseph, the earthly father of Jesus, through dreams. An angel appeared to him in different dreams to deliver wisdom as to what he should do, directing him to marry Mary and get her and baby Jesus out of Bethlehem when Herod sought to kill Him.

An open vision is when someone sees the vision with open eyes as if in a movie theater or it can feel like the person is actually there where the vision is taking place. Open visions and messages delivered by angels are usually important information. I see mostly pictures or visions in my mind. These pictures often occur when I am praying or during worship.

Discovering the Holy Spirit

Not all pictures that we see are from God. We have an imagination and can rehearse stories and scenarios in our minds. I have learned to sanctify my imagination and be careful what I watch on television or in the movies, because it will influence what I see.

At times I pray prayers of cleansing, asking the Holy Spirit to wash me from anything that could hinder me from receiving from God. If I feel a vision is demonic I pray a cleansing prayer over myself, and ask the Holy Spirit if there is something I did wrong or something I watched that could have influenced me to see visions from the enemy. If the Holy Spirit shows me something, that is good. Otherwise I pray like this, "Wash me, Holy Spirit, cleanse my mind. I take authority over any demonic spirits coming against my mind in Jesus' name. I want to receive everything God has for me." If I am unsure about something I put it on the shelf, figuratively speaking. If it is from God He will confirm it. I have learned that God has many, many ways He can speak to us. If it is really important, He will get your attention. The key is to stay open. We can also set healthy boundaries in the spirit. It is good to pray this way, "I only want to receive from You, Holy Spirit, what God wants me to see or know. I don't receive demonic visions or revelation, in Jesus' name."

When God speak to us through a vision, a picture we see in our mind, or a dream, it is often in parable form and we need to interpret it. A young friend who I pick up from school had a funny dream about me. She said I was driving a car and she and two of her friends from school were in the car. Suddenly her friend Isaiah was behind the wheel driving the car. My friend said that was crazy because Isaiah was only six years old! We both laughed about this crazy dream. As I was pondering this dream, I realized in the Bible Isaiah was a prophet and if the car is symbolic of my life, then Isaiah was symbolic of the prophetic. Hearing God's voice gives me direction and sometimes surprising things have happened in my journey. On the surface we laughed about the crazy dream, but when I thought about it, its true meaning unfolded.

A dream or a vision is symbolic, like a riddle or a parable. I look at the symbols in the dream. Why is this specific person in the dream? Does the name have a significant meaning or is it because of what the person does? When I have dreams with one specific son in it, I know it has a connection to prayer, and when my other son is in the dream, it often has a connection to evangelism—that is, if the dreams aren't about them personally. God speaks to us in the symbols and ways we will understand.

I had a dream about a big room that looked like a dining hall. There were round tables with chairs and a sitting area with chairs, sofas, and tables. There was an opening in the wall where food could be served from the kitchen. Seven years after I had the dream I started to write *Discovering God*. That dream helped me to decide to write in a way that it could be used in small groups. I understood this from the food being delivered to areas where people sat comfortably and chatted. For a long time I didn't really understand the dream. I knew there was something in it, but the understanding came later when I needed it.

"For God speaks again and again, though people do not recognize it. He speaks in dreams, in visions of the night, when deep sleep falls on people as they lie in their beds" (Job 33:14-15 NLT). In my early years as a Christian, I dreamed but didn't realize that God could speak to me through dreams. Of course, not every dream is from God. We process what happens to us in life through dreams too. I write down the dreams that I remember. For some I press in and ask God for the interpretation, but others just don't make sense. If the dream is important, you will wonder what it means and it will hold your attention until you find out what it means.

I don't make decisions based on one dream. God will say the same thing in two or three different ways to bring confirmation—especially if it is a big adjustment like changing a job or moving to a different city. If we interpret a dream wrongly we can miss God's will. In 2001 we just moved into our house and I had a dream that the house we were living in was not our final destination; we were just in transition and the house we were going to live in was on the top of a mountain. It was hidden and surrounded by trees. In the natural we just bought a house. If I had interpreted it that we were living in the wrong house, it would have been the wrong interpretation. Most of the time dreams from God have a spiritual interpretation. I keep all revelation from God with an open hand and allow Him to move upon it in His timing. Looking back at that dream, it could have pointed to my involvement with our house of prayer. A mountain also refers to the presence of God, "Who may climb the mountain of the Lord? Who may stand in his holy place?" (Psalm 24:3 NLT). This dream could refer to a person's private devotional time, meaning that God has a secret place for us that is like this house hidden high up on a mountain.

The Bible says, "The Lord spoke to Moses face to face, as a man speaks to his friend" (Exodus 33:11). When I read this I say, *oh, I want God to speak to me like this*. If I look at the level of obedience God required of Moses, I hesitate a bit. When God told Moses to hit the rock with the stick, he had to obey or there would be consequences for disobedience. They had to follow God's exact instructions in the building of the tabernacle, in how they brought sacrifices, and in worship.

God has given us the Ten Commandments to obey and much wisdom in His Word. Obeying those will help us to lead a good life. God has a best plan for each one of us. We find that plan by seeking God and praying and telling Him we desire that plan. God knows the gifts, the talents, and the training each person has. He will bring guidance as to where to apply for a job or grant an unexpected connection with someone. There are very few things in my life that God has very clearly directed me or my husband to do. We keep our hearts open and desire His best plan for our lives. We continue to pray and act on what we feel He has put in our hearts and we explore open doors. As we do this, we trust God that He will help us make the right decisions and tell us if we don't.

God is attracted to hunger and obedience. Think about it this way: you attend a church and notice a person who you would like to become friends with, but every time you approach them they turn away and ignore you. Most people would soon give up and not try to become friends. God doesn't give up on us, but those who respect Him and desire to hear His voice and be in relationship with Him receive more than those who don't really care about Him. He allows you to practice in little things. Obey Him in the little things and you will see good fruit come forth through small acts of daily obedience.

Hermie Reynolds

Discussion Questions: How Do I Hear the Holy Spirit?

1. Do you think the Holy Spirit wants to speak to you? Discuss.

_____
_____
_____
_____
_____
_____

2. Think about your life. How do you learn spiritual lessons? Share how you learn life lessons—by making mistakes, from reading books, from listening to other people.

_____
_____
_____
_____
_____

3. Underline the ways God speaks to you—from the Bible, through other people, songs, dreams, visions, life situations, impressions, etc. If there are other ways God speaks to you, add them to the list. Allow time to share about the ways you have experienced God's guidance.

_____
_____
_____
_____
_____
_____

Discovering the Holy Spirit

4. Discuss the importance of the following in hearing the Holy Spirit:
   - "Holding your hand open" when you feel God speaking to you. This means to not hold on so tightly to what God speaks to you that your life falls apart if it doesn't come to pass or if you heard wrong.
   - Receiving counsel from friends when you make a big decision.
   - God's timing.

   _____
   _____
   _____

5. Read the Bible passage below and ask the Holy Spirit to speak to you about a phrase or part of this Scripture. Read it in your own Bible too.

   > "The law always ended up being used as a Band-Aid on sin instead of a deep healing of it. And now what the law code asked for but we couldn't deliver is accomplished as we, instead of redoubling our efforts, simply embrace what the Spirit is doing in us. ...But if God himself has taken up residence in your life, you can hardly be thinking more of yourself than of him. Anyone, of course, who has not welcomed this invisible but clearly present God, the Spirit of Christ, won't know what we're talking about. But for you who welcome Him, in whom He dwells—even though you still experience all the limitations of sin—you yourself experience life on God's terms. ...So don't you see that we don't owe this old do-it-yourself life one red cent. There's nothing in it for us, nothing at all. The best thing to do is give it a decent burial and get on with your new life. God's Spirit beckons. There are things to do and places to go! This resurrection life you received from God is not a timid, grave-tending life. It is adventurously expectant, greeting God with a childlike, 'What's next, Papa?' God's Spirit touches our spirits and confirms who we really are" (Romans 8:4, 9-15 MSG).

Chapter 11: Walking in the Fullness of the Holy Spirit

"The Spirit of the Lord shall rest upon Him, the Spirit of wisdom and understanding, the Spirit of counsel and might, the Spirit of knowledge and of the fear of the Lord" (Isaiah 11:2).

When Jesus was baptized in the Jordan River, the heavens opened and God the Father said, "This is My beloved Son, in whom I am well pleased" (Matthew 3:17). The Holy Spirit came down like a dove, settled, and remained upon Jesus. Isaiah 11:2 says, "The Spirit of the Lord shall rest upon Him"; the Hebrew word for *rest* means to "rest, settle down and remain."[14] Psalm 104:3 tells us that God wraps Himself or covers Himself with light. The Holy Spirit came down and rested on Jesus, empowering Him to walk in the power of the Spirit to do miracles and heal people.

In Isaiah's prophecy we read Jesus' mission: "The Spirit of the Lord God is upon Me, Because the Lord has anointed Me to preach good tidings to the poor; He has sent Me to heal the brokenhearted, to proclaim liberty to the captives, and the opening of the prison to those who are bound" (Isaiah 61:1). This empowering of the Holy Spirit came upon Jesus after His baptism and remained on Him. The Holy Spirit led Jesus into the desert where He fasted for forty days, and He came out of it and did His first miracle at the wedding in Cana (John 2:1-11). I have read many biographies of men and women who walked in great ministries. Most of them had some kind of an encounter with God that changed their lives and

---

14. Brown, Driver, Briggs, and Gesenius. "Hebrew Lexicon entry for *nuwach*," The KJV Old Testament Hebrew Lexicon, accessed March 1, 2015, http://www.biblestudytools.com/lexicons/hebrew/kjv/nuwach.html.

Discovering the Holy Spirit

direction and thrust them into the call of God. God works in each of us; we can trust Him to anoint us for what He is calling us to do.

I have heard the phrase "with the appointing comes the anointing," meaning that if God calls a person to do a task, He also equips and anoints the person for the job. The craftsmen who built the tabernacle were anointed by the Holy Spirit to do the job. God had filled Bezalel, "with the Spirit of God, in wisdom and understanding, in knowledge and all manner of workmanship, to design artistic works, to work in gold and silver and bronze, in cutting jewels for setting, in carving wood, and to work in all manner of artistic workmanship. And He has put in his heart the ability to teach" (Exodus 35:31-34). When God calls us to do something, He will use our natural gifts and He will empower us to accomplish that call. It will not be accomplished by striving and working in our own strength.

After I became a born-again Christian, I had a great desire to know truth and a strong hunger to know God. I know He put that hunger inside of me. It was all grace. We just follow and obey. He can accomplish great things with a yielded, willing vessel (Daniel 11:32). "It is God who enables us, along with you, to stand firm for Christ. He has commissioned us and he has identified us as his own by placing the Holy Spirit in our hearts as the first installment that guarantees everything he has promised us" (2 Corinthians 1:21-22 NLT).

Jesus not only walked in the miracle-working power of God, but He had wisdom in every situation, understanding about the Scriptures, counsel from the Holy Spirit to do the right thing in every situation, and supernatural knowledge from the Holy Spirit. He also walked in obedience to God in the reverential fear of the Lord. He indeed had the Spirit without limit (John 3:34). Jesus not only had supernatural power, He also had everything He needed to live a godly and holy life through the Holy Spirit. Jesus affected every person He met.

The word *Spirit* is the Hebrew word *ruwach* which means Spirit of God, wind of heaven, breath of God.[15] It is the same word that was used

---

15. Brown, Driver, Briggs, and Gesenius. "Hebrew Lexicon entry for *ruwach*," The KJV Old Testament Hebrew Lexicon, accessed March 1, 2015, http://www.biblestudytools.com/lexicons/hebrew/kjv/ruwach-2.html.

in Genesis 1 where the Spirit of God was brooding over the earth. The same word is used in Genesis 41:38 where Joseph interpreted Pharaoh's dreams and Pharaoh said it was obvious that the *ruwach* was in Joseph. It's amazing to think that the same Holy Spirit who was in Jesus is in us too. "I pray that you will begin to understand how incredibly great his power is to help those who believe him. It is that same mighty power" (Ephesians 1:19 TLB).

The Spirit of the Lord

The Hebrew word used for *Lord* in Isaiah 11:2, "The Spirit of the Lord shall rest upon Him," is *Yehovah*. It is the proper name for God and means "the existing One."[16] When God revealed Himself to Moses and said "I am who I am" (Exodus 3:14), He used the word *hayah* which means "to be or to exist."[17] The Spirit of God who was upon Joseph giving him favor, who gave the craftsmen the skills to build the tabernacle, the One who was upon Samson giving him strength and who was upon the Old Testament prophets giving them the word of the Lord—that same Spirit was upon Jesus. John the Baptist said about Jesus, "For he is sent by God. He speaks God's words, for God gives him the Spirit without limit. The Father loves his Son and has put everything into his hands. And anyone who believes in God's Son has eternal life. Anyone who doesn't obey the Son will never experience eternal life but remains under God's angry judgment" (John 3:34-36 NLT).

Jesus was worthy of the tremendous trust God placed in His hands. He gave Him the Spirit without limit and great authority, saying that those who didn't obey Him would be under God's judgment. A teacher once shared that from heaven's perspective, God's home, heaven, is holy and pure. If people could enter heaven with their sins, then it would not be holy anymore, but the same as the earth. To keep it holy and free from sin, there had to be something to protect it from sin. The blood of Jesus is that protective barrier. We can only enter through

---

16. Brown, Driver, Briggs, and Gesenius. "Hebrew Lexicon entry for *Yehovah*," The KJV Old Testament Hebrew Lexicon, accessed March 1,2015, http://www.biblestudytools.com/lexicons/hebrew/kjv/yehovah.html.

17. Ibid., "Hebrew Lexicon entry for *hayah*," The KJV Old Testament Hebrew Lexicon, accessed March 1, 2015, http://www.biblestudytools.com/lexicons/hebrew/kjv/hayah.html.

the blood of Jesus that washes us clean and keeps heaven without sin, filled with joy and peace, holy and full of the wonderment of the awe of God.

Jesus could walk in the full measure of the Spirit because He laid down His life to obey the will of His Father. Jesus came from the throne room of God, the place of glory with His Father in heaven (John 17:5), to earth where He became a humble servant of humanity. He did not come down as a king to sit on an earthly throne. He could have come down from heaven with millions of angels, kicked the Roman government out, and become a king. He came as a man, as a carpenter's son, and because of his willingness to leave that place of glory and humble Himself, being willing to die the same death as a criminal, God exalted Him and gave Jesus the name above all names; and everyone in heaven, on earth, and under the earth will bow their knees before Him (Philippians 2:5-11). This is the reason Jesus walked in the full measure of the Holy Spirit. When Jesus was not honored in His hometown and was seen according to the flesh instead as Mary and Joseph's son, and the people did not honor the presence of the Holy Spirit that was upon Him, He didn't do many miracles (Mark 6:3-5). Isn't it amazing that when Jesus prayed for the church He said:

> "That they all may be one, [just] as You, Father, are in Me and I in You, that they also may be one in Us, so that the world may believe and be convinced that You have sent Me. I have given to them the glory and honor which You have given Me, that they may be one [even] as We are one: I in them and You in Me, in order that they may become one and perfectly united, that the world may know and [definitely] recognize that You sent Me and that You have loved them [even] as You have loved Me" (John 17:21-23 AMP).

The glory that was upon Jesus is upon His church. There is much more that we can walk in and access if we come to realize these treasures and truths of the Word and start walking in them (Colossians 2:3).

Hermie Reynolds

The Spirit of Wisdom and Understanding

How do we gain wisdom? Proverbs provides the answer, "How does a man become wise? The first step is to trust and reverence the Lord!" (Proverbs 1:7 TLB). Other translations read that the fear of the Lord is the beginning of wisdom. The fear of the Lord means to have reverence and respect for God. We will not listen to and obey someone we don't respect. When my kids began to make some decisions by themselves I was a bit concerned when I didn't fully agree with a decision. God is like a wise parent too. The only difference is He really does have the best answers every time, and He has the wisdom that will help us make the right decisions every time too.

Where does wisdom come from? "For the Lord gives skillful and godly Wisdom; from His mouth come knowledge and understanding" (Proverbs 2:6 AMP). The Living Bible calls wisdom a treasure. How we need God's wisdom in our lives and in our relationships with others! We find these treasures as we walk with the Holy Spirit, learn from the Bible, and receive wisdom from God as we seek Him. What does God's wisdom do? It protects us from the traps of the enemy, leads us on the right path, guards us, and helps us discern between what is right and what is wrong; it also helps us make wise decisions. The result of a word of wisdom is that it brings truth. The moment when the light goes on and we see truth, we suddenly have a clearer picture of what is going on in a situation or we know what is the right decision for a situation (Proverbs 2:6-10).

More keys to this are found in Proverbs 3:19-20: "The Lord by wisdom founded the earth; by understanding He established the heavens; by His knowledge the depths were broken up, and clouds drop down the dew." God founded the earth with wisdom. Imagine for a moment that God has given a group of engineers the task to come forth with a plan to create the universe. All of the scientific world—engineers, medical doctors, biologists, psychologists, etc.—would not be able to come up with such a perfect creation as the earth God created. The exact tilt of the earth and its distance from the moon and sun would have to be perfect to sustain life on earth. Those are very exact mathematic calculations. God used wisdom, understanding, and knowledge to create the earth.

Discovering the Holy Spirit

We gain knowledge from our parents, school, and church. Upon that knowledge, we can build with wisdom and understanding. If we only learn knowledge, we forget it easily; it is better to understand what we have learned, then we can apply it in wisdom. It is the same with the Bible. We can gain knowledge from the Bible, but the Holy Spirit brings revelation (Ephesians 1:17-19). The Holy Spirit can give us wisdom in situations; He can tell us when to speak and when to be silent. He showed Jesus when to be silent and when to speak when He was before His accusers (Luke 23:9; Matthew 27:11-14).

One of my sons told me he had a conversation with his friend and suddenly knew three things that he needed to share with him. It was information he knew God gave him, because it wasn't something that he had known before. That is how the Holy Spirit can share wisdom with us to share with someone else. The more we hear His voice, the more we grow in discerning when it is God and when it is us. At times this can happen so naturally that we may not realize it was the Holy Spirit. Later when we think about the conversation, we recognize that the Holy Spirit had directed what we had said. This is one of the ways the Holy Spirit answers our prayer that He would come and direct our conversations. It is so easy to mix what the Holy Spirit is saying with my own thoughts that I don't tell people, *this is what the Holy Spirit is saying.* I let them discern and pray about it on their own. I also don't give directive advice. Each person is responsible before God for their own lives and they have to make their own decisions. Often the Holy Spirit will remind me of a situation I walked through and what happened and direct me to share that with someone. The Holy Spirit has wisdom for each person in their own situation.

Jesus received supernatural wisdom from His Father. When Jesus told a paralyzed man that his sins were forgiven, He knew what the religious leaders were thinking. "Jesus knew immediately what they were thinking, so he asked them, 'Why do you question this in your hearts?'" (Mark 2:8 NLT). He did not answer their questions. He only answered when He was questioned about who He was. He had wisdom to know when to speak and when to be silent.

Jesus waited three days before he went to Lazarus' family after He received the news that Lazarus had died (John 11). In John 7 we see the Jews had begun plotting to kill Jesus, so Jesus stayed behind and did not go to the Feast of Tabernacles, but halfway through the feast He showed up and began to preach. Why the sudden change of mind? It must have been in response to the Holy Spirit. God knew when the time was that Jesus would be captured so the Holy Spirit kept Jesus safe until the right time came. Jesus knew when to wait and when to go.

The Spirit of Counsel and Might

The Hebrew word for "counsel" is `etsah which means counsel, advice, or purpose.[18] Jesus walked in the counsel, advice, and purpose of the Holy Spirit. He didn't just wander around the Judean area randomly, but followed God's instructions delivered by the Holy Spirit. He had divine appointments with people. The meeting with the woman at the well in John 4 was a divine Holy Spirit appointment. Jesus spoke to one woman and a whole village was affected. He modeled for us how to live. He was a man walking and living on earth, empowered by the Holy Spirit. Jesus is not here anymore; we are His hands and His feet to show people how Jesus would have treated them.

The Hebrew word for "might" is the word *gabuwrah* which means might, bravery, strength, or mighty deeds.[19] The Spirit of Might came upon Samson and he killed a lion (Judges 14:6) and later killed thirty of the men of Ashkelon (Judges 14:19). There are many instances that you read, "Then the Spirit of the Lord came upon him (Samson) mightily" (Judges 14:19), and he showed extraordinary strength. Where Jesus turned over the tables in the temple, nobody resisted Him. This could have been a demonstration of the Spirit of Might, but He was also gripped by the Holy Spirit's passion and zeal for His Father's house—that it should be a house of prayer. Most of His life Jesus walked in humility, meekness, and compassion. He had all strength and power available to

18. Brown, Driver, Briggs, and Gesenius. "Hebrew Lexicon entry for `etsah," The KJV Old Testament Hebrew Lexicon, accessed March 1, 2015, http://www.biblestudytools.com/lexicons/hebrew/kjv/etsah-2.html.
19. Ibid., "Hebrew Lexicon entry for *gabuwrah*," The KJV Old Testament Hebrew Lexicon, accessed March 1, 2015, http://www.biblestudytools.com/lexicons/hebrew/kjv/gebuwrah.html.

Him, but He knew He was not on earth to establish an earthly kingdom and raise up an earthly army. He came to accomplish the purposes of God. He laid down that power for a greater reward—to save humanity.

The Spirit of Knowledge

The Hebrew word for *knowledge* is *da`ath*, and it means knowledge, perception, skill, discernment, understanding, wisdom.[20] The Spirit of Knowledge gave the craftsmen the skill to build the tabernacle (Exodus 35:30-33). All our gifts and talents comes from God: "Every good gift and every perfect gift is from above, and comes down from the Father of lights" (James 1:17). My husband enjoyed math and science in school and became an engineer. Even though he went to college to get the skills and knowledge to do his job, there have been many times where he has come across a problem that was seemingly without solution. The Holy Spirit has helped him and given Him answers to problems at work. We have the Holy Spirit. We can ask for help when we need Him. There have been times that my husband had a sudden thought to check a specific component on a project and that was exactly where the problem was. Other times it took longer, but he has solved many seemingly impossible problems with the help of the Holy Spirit.

The Spirit of Knowledge usually operates through the preacher in church meetings. They will know what sickness the Lord wants to heal. Sometimes a person on a prayer team will get a pain in the area where the sickness that needs to be prayed for is. The Spirit of Knowledge brings supernatural knowledge of a situation which a person hasn't been told about. We can receive knowledge from the Holy Spirit through a dream, a sudden insight, seeing someone who reminds us of a friend, a thought, or many other ways. A friend shared with me how two people contacted her one week and said they were praying for her. She said that one of them was a lady she had not heard from for six years! The Lord laid my friend on this person's heart for that certain time. Usually the

---

20. Brown, Driver, Briggs and Gesenius. "Hebrew Lexicon entry for *da`ath*," The KJV Old Testament Hebrew Lexicon, Accessed March 1, 2015, http://www.biblestudytools.com/lexicons/hebrew/kjv/daath.html.

Holy Spirit alerts me to pray for this friend but that particular week I had a lot on my plate so the Holy Spirit nudged others to pray for her.

The Fear of the Lord

The fear of the Lord does not refer to being afraid of God; it means to have respect and reverence for God because He is so much bigger than we are. The church that I grew up in had a reverent, worshipful awe of God. I am thankful that I learned that from my childhood. A lack of respect for God comes from a lack of knowledge about who He is. If we know how majestic in power and authority He is, we will honor and respect Him. The Bible has a wonderful promise for those who fear the Lord, "The secret [of the sweet, satisfying companionship] of the Lord have they who fear (revere and worship) Him, and He will show them His covenant and reveal to them its [deep, inner] meaning" (Psalm 25:14 AMP). Those who honor and respect God have the invitation of living in a close relationship with Him. Enoch lived in such a relationship, "And Enoch walked [in habitual fellowship] with God; and he was not, for God took him [home with Him] (Genesis 5:24 AMP). Abraham, Moses, David, and others also walked in close fellowship with God.

Obedience to God shows in the way we honor and respect Him. If we see a child who is disrespectful and disobedient to their parent, we know that it shouldn't be that way. Honor, love, and respect from a pure heart leads to blessing. We are God's children and although He has invited us into a friendship relationship, it is not without respect. There are many promises attached to the fear of the Lord. Long life is one of them (Proverbs 10:27). The fear of the Lord is to hate evil (Proverbs 8:13). We don't hate people; God loves people. Jesus showed God's love in the parable of the Prodigal Son, where this dad waited for his son to return. We need the fear of the Lord, the hatred of evil in our own lives, to keep us from sinning. The fear of the Lord is exemplified by living in obedience to God. "If you keep My commandments, you will abide in My love, just as I have kept My Father's commandments and abide in His love" (John 15:10).

The Holy Spirit as a Fire

We see different types of symbolism for the Holy Spirit. In some Scriptures, He is compared to a fire. John the Baptist said he baptized people in water, but Jesus would baptize them with the Holy Spirit and fire (Matthew 3:11). When we encounter the Holy Spirit, He sets our hearts on fire and stirs our hearts with a greater love for Jesus. What does a fire do? It burns, it consumes. The fire of the Holy Spirit burns away or consumes the dross in our lives—all the things that hold us back and prevent us from becoming wholehearted and passionate for Jesus. This happens when we walk through a difficult situation. When we gave away and sold all our furniture before we left South Africa, I can remember feeling like I was walking off a cliff. I had no idea what it was going to be like on the other side. I had never been to the United States before, and here I was moving there. But Jesus was on the other side of the cliff, waiting for me.

A fire burns, and encountering the Holy Spirit will cause our hearts to burn with love for Jesus. Song of Songs 8:7 says, "Many waters cannot quench love, nor can the floods drown it. If a man would give for love all the wealth of his house, it would be utterly despised." This is a fire that cannot be put out. The Holy Spirit is the One who works in our hearts to stir our hearts to fall more deeply in love with Jesus. It is a love that has caused many to die the death of a martyr. Even in the face of persecution or death, this love burns stronger than the fear of death. I have heard that in the persecuted church, they pray that persecution will come to the American church, because it was in the face of persecution that the church grew most.

A fire spreads and is difficult to contain. The Holy Spirit empowers us to want to tell others about Jesus. Imagine if we all had a spiritual fire on the inside and we gathered together. We would have a big bonfire! When we gather together with other believers, it strengthens our faith. We feel encouraged and the fire burns brighter in our own hearts. If we are isolated and alone, it is more challenging to keep the fire burning brightly. A coal that is taken out of the fire dies after a while. I have received very timely words of encouragement through friends at church, and at times through e-mail or even social media. God wants to keep us on fire for Him.

John the Baptist said of Jesus, "He will baptize you with the Holy Spirit and fire" (Matthew 3:11). In Acts tongues of fire come upon those in the upper room (Acts 2:3). The result of this was that the disciples preached the gospel and 3,000 people were saved. "A fire shall always be burning on the altar; it shall never go out" (Leviticus 6:13). Just as the fire on the altar was kept going by adding coals, there are things I can do to stir the Holy Spirit fire in my heart. I often listen to Christian radio when I drive. I try to read my Bible and pray daily and set aside time to connect with God. The glory of the Lord is also compared to a fire. "The sight of the glory of the Lord was like a consuming fire on the top of the mountain in the eyes of the children of Israel" (Exodus 24:17). Fire gives light in darkness, and it can spread; the believers in the book of Acts spread the gospel message that Jesus was alive and many became believers.

In Malachi 3:2 we find the picture of a refiner's fire. "For He is like a refiner's fire and like launderers' soap." To refine metals, the raw material must be heated until it melts. This causes the impurities in the metal to separate and rise to the surface. The impurities are skimmed off. The process is repeated until the pure metal comes forth. A metallurgist can see his reflection as the metal becomes pure.[21] In our walk with God He takes us through this process more than once. His desire is that the reflection of His Son will be seen in us. Early in my walk with Jesus, I learned to keep short accounts with God, to repent quickly when I did something wrong. I have experienced His refiner's fire most in the area of my emotions. When He came and revealed an area of rejection or wounding or a performance-driven orientation, He came and brought healing and change. The Holy Spirit is committed and determined to change us to become more like Jesus. "The Spirit Whom He has caused to dwell in us yearns over us and He yearns for the Spirit [to be welcome] with a jealous love" (James 4:5 AMP).

Jesus used the picture of water when He told the disciples about the Holy Spirit, "'He who believes in Me, as the Scripture has said, out of his heart will flow rivers of living water.' But this He spoke concerning the Spirit, whom those believing in Him would receive" (John 7:38-39). I can often feel the power and presence of the Holy Spirit when a person puts their hand on my shoulder to pray for me. It is that flow of living Holy

---

21. "Footnote to Malachi 3:3" *The Life Application Bible*, Wheaton, Illinois: Tyndale House, 1986, 1313.

Discovering the Holy Spirit

Spirit water from the person to me. Even if someone doesn't touch me, I still experience the power of the Holy Spirit when someone prays for me.

Once we had many house guests. For several weeks at a time I went to the house of prayer and felt a bit tired and empty. I sat in the presence of God, praying and focusing on Ephesians 3:16: "May He grant you out of the rich treasury of His glory to be strengthened and reinforced with mighty power in the inner man by the [Holy] Spirit [Himself indwelling your innermost being and personality]" (AMP). I continued to pray that God would wash weariness and the care of the world from me. I focused on short phrases from the Scripture. It didn't feel like much happened, but later when I walked out, I realized how much better I felt. The burdens had lifted. I felt refreshed and joyful. I had a drink of living water; the Holy Spirit had filled me and I had living water to give to others.

The Holy Spirit is also compared to the wind. In Acts 2 the Holy Spirit came like a powerful mighty wind. Ezekiel saw a valley of dry bones in a vision and prophecy to Israel. "Then he told me to call to the wind and say: 'The Lord God says: Come from the four winds, O Spirit, and breathe upon these slain bodies, that they may live again'" (Ezekiel 37:9 TLB). The result of the Holy Spirit coming would be an army raised up for God and people receiving new hearts of compassion. We too need the Holy Spirit to come awaken and bring spiritual life to people. Jesus compared our lives as born-again believers to the wind. "The wind blows where it wishes, and you hear the sound of it, but cannot tell where it comes from and where it goes. So is everyone who is born of the Spirit" (John 3:8). When we have the Holy Spirit in us He will lead us, and it will be like the wind; you do not know which way it will blow. It doesn't mean that we don't plan, but we make room for the leading and guidance of the Holy Spirit.

Jesus said, speaking of the Holy Spirit, "And when He has come" (John 16:8). He did not refer to the Holy Spirit as "it." Even though the Holy Spirit doesn't have a physical body, He has the characteristics of a person. A person can think, feel, reason, have emotions, and can make decisions. We see this of the Holy Spirit too, "no one can know God's thoughts except God's own Spirit" (1 Corinthians 2:11 NLT). What a privilege that we have the One who knows God's thoughts living on the inside of us. The Holy Spirit can feel. We read that He can be grieved, "Don't grieve God. Don't break his heart. His Holy Spirit, moving and breathing in you, is the most intimate part of your life, making you fit for himself. Don't take such a gift for granted" (Ephesians 4:30 MSG).

In Acts 5:3, Ananias and his wife, Sapphira, sold a piece of land. Ananias brought part of the money to the apostles, telling them it was the full amount. Peter confronted him and told him that he didn't have to give any of the money to them. It was his own choice to sell the property and to keep or give away the money, but Ananias lied to the Holy Spirit (Acts 5:3 KJV). When Ananias heard this, he fell to the ground and instantly died. His wife came in a little bit later with the same story, and she died instantly too (Acts 5:1-10). You can imagine how this affected the other believers. They felt the fear of the Lord—*whatever you do, do not lie to the Holy Spirit.*

"Don't be drunk with wine, because that will ruin your life. Instead, be filled with the Holy Spirit" (Ephesians 5:18 NLT). To be drunk with wine ruins a person's life, but to be filled with the Holy Spirit brings life. The Message describes it this way "Drink the Spirit of God, huge draughts of him." How do we do that? Spending time in worship is one of the easiest ways to be filled or drink from the Holy Spirit. When we really enter in and connect with the Holy Spirit, a time of fellowship or communion happens.

I have experienced this driving in the car too. A song will come on Christian radio and suddenly I feel my spirit is filled with joy and I am connecting with God. As we sing God's truths about God's love and the victory we have in Jesus, we are filled with hope, and we experience a time of being filled with the Spirit of God. I need to "drink" or spend time in the presence of God; otherwise I become spiritually empty and lose my peace and joy. Praying or reading our Bibles can also be a time of connecting with the Holy Spirit.

Discussion Questions: Walking in the Fullness of the Holy Spirit

1. Look up one of these Scriptures about wisdom and write down what do you learn from it (Proverbs 2:6-10; 8:11; 11:2; 15:33; 16:16; Ephesians 1:17; Colossians 2:2-3; James 1:5; 3:17). Share what you learn about wisdom from these Scriptures.

2. What is the connection between wisdom and understanding (Psalm 49:3)?

3. Jesus is not here anymore; we are His hands and His feet to show people how Jesus would have treated them. How would it affect the way you treat others if you kept in mind that you are revealing Jesus to those around you through how you act and what you do?

4. Share some thoughts around how we partner with the Holy Spirit. How do we recognize what He is doing and work with Him?

_____
_____
_____
_____
_____

5. Take some time to ponder this Scripture. You can focus on part of the Scripture or slowly go through the whole thing. You can also read Scriptures that connect to this. Let the Holy Spirit lead you.

> "For the Lord grants wisdom! His every word is a treasure of knowledge and understanding. He grants good sense to the godly—His saints. He is their shield, protecting them and guarding their pathway. He shows how to distinguish right from wrong, how to find the right decision every time. For wisdom and truth will enter the very center of your being, filling your life with joy" (Proverbs 2:6-10 TLB).

Chapter 12: Growing in the Holy Spirit

"You are living a brand new kind of life that is continually learning more and more of what is right, and trying constantly to be more and more like Christ who created this new life within you" (Colossians 3:10 TLB).

When I look at creation, I am amazed at how detailed and specific God has made different plants and animals. Have you ever thought about a giraffe's long neck? I wonder how they sleep. They would be very vulnerable when they lay down that long neck. Look at a beautiful, delicate butterfly. That butterfly was a once an earthbound worm that only lived to eat. Eventually it was transformed. The butterfly had to struggle to get out of its chrysalis. If a person cuts it open to help the butterfly, its wings will not be strong enough to fly. The butterfly needs to go through the struggle to develop the strength in their wings to fly. There are times when our struggles are hard. We would like God to pour out blessings over us and that is His desire, but He knows that without the struggle, we won't be able to mount up as eagles and live life strong in the spirit. Just like the worm that eats a lot before it is transformed into the butterfly, we need spiritual food to grow spiritually.

The Amplified Bible describe this transformation in this way: "And have clothed yourselves with the new [spiritual self], which is [ever in the process of being] renewed and remolded into [fuller and more perfect knowledge upon] knowledge after the image [the likeness] of Him who created it" (Colossians 3:10 AMP). This is the journey we are going through in life—being transformed to be more like Jesus. We want to live like Jesus and love like Him. It is a process which would be hard to go through alone. But we are not alone. We are part of a family. It is a great blessing to me to have Christian friends to pray with me when I am going through difficulties. Receiving helpful or encouraging words from my brethren can give me insight into my situation.

Jesus said, "I am the bread of life" (John 6:48). In the tabernacle, the Holy Place had a table with showbread (Exodus 25:23-29; Numbers 4:7) and a lampstand for lighting up the room (Exodus 25:31-39). The bread was called the bread of His Presence, and it is symbolic of Jesus and the Word; the lampstand is symbolic of the Holy Spirit. The Holy Spirit is the One who draws us into the presence of God and opens the Word to us. The Bible is sometimes read as a history book, "You search the Scriptures, for you believe they give you eternal life. And the Scriptures point to me! Yet, you won't come to me so that I can give you this life eternal!" (John 5:39 TLB).

We miss a great deal if we read the Bible as a history book. We can meet a *living person* in the pages of that book! We can meet Jesus in the Bible as we read it. The Word is a man, Jesus Christ, and the Holy Spirit, the Lampstand, is the One who illuminates or reveals Jesus in the Scriptures to us. He is the Spirit of wisdom and revelation that Ephesians 1:17 talks about. Therefore I ask the Holy Spirit to reveal the Word to me, and to speak to me when I read the Bible. When we spend time with Jesus reading the Bible and time in worship, it is like eating spiritual food.

We are bombarded by cultural images of success in the media—women with perfect bodies, neat material possessions, and dream vacations—the best things in life that money can buy. God's focus is not on outward appearances and possessions. I am thankful that He looks at us in a different way. When Samuel went to Jesse's house to anoint one of his sons to become the next king of Israel, God told him, "Do not look at his appearance or at his physical stature, because I have refused him. For the Lord does not see as man sees; for man looks at the outward appearance, but the Lord looks at the heart" (1 Samuel 16:7). This doesn't mean that we should neglect our appearance, but it does mean that our outer appearance should not be our focal point.

The mind is the control center from where we do things. When we're awake, our minds think and constantly process information. The mind is like the hard disk of a computer. When we become born again, we don't get a new hard disk, but the Bible says we should be transformed in the way we think (Romans 12:2). What we have learned in life does not always line up with the truth of the Word. We have to be reeducated and renewed in the truth of God's Word.

The Bible is a treasure. We need to appropriate this treasure daily. In Bible school our sons had to read a certain number of chapters in the Bible every day. I can see the good fruit it produced to have both spiritual discipline and a Holy Spirit environment. This is vital to our growth. Our natural thinking does not line up with the Bible. The natural mind fights for its own self-preservation, comfort, and well-being, whereas God wants us to make right decisions based on biblical principles and wisdom. He measures growth in character and spiritual depth and maturity.

The Holy Spirit didn't come to control us. He came to teach, lead, and guide us. He is a Friend who is closer than a brother or sister. The Holy Spirit is always in agreement with God, who gave us a free will, so He will not manipulate and control us. He is powerful enough and could control us if He wanted, but He honors man's free will. The impressions that the Holy Spirit brings are not in a loud booming voice, but a feeling or a thought that can easily be ignored. "Therefore take heed how you hear. For whoever has, to him more will be given; and whoever does not have, even what he seems to have will be taken from him" (Luke 8:18).

One summer our oldest son struggled for weeks to get a job. He heard that a restaurant was hiring and applied. He didn't hear back from them, so he decided to stop by and see the manager. The manager kept him waiting for two hours, but my son persevered and waited patiently. When the manager talked to him, he hired him. He found out later that this manager let people wait to see how desperate they were for a job. The Holy Spirit can help us to find a job, find a solution for a problem, give us direction, warn us of danger, prevent accidents, and so much more if we will hear His voice and obey.

Romans 8:27 says the Holy Spirit prays God's will for us, "And the Father who knows all hearts knows what the Spirit is saying, for the Spirit pleads for us believers in harmony with God's own will" (NLT). Holy Spirit is our teacher; He knows what we need to learn to

Discovering the Holy Spirit

be equipped to accomplish the task God has for us on earth. Our time here on earth is not the end of all things; this is only preparation for an eternity with God. Abraham and Moses were friends of God. We have this time on earth to develop our friendship with God, and we have a Helper to do that called the Holy Spirit who will lead and guide us. He comforts us in times of trouble and gives us peace. He is the One who reminds us of Scriptures when we need them (John 14:26-27 AMP).

When Jesus was baptized, the Holy Spirit came upon Him like a dove. We often see the dove as the symbol of the Holy Spirit. I was listening to messages about the Holy Spirit and thought that the picture of a dove did not fit Him right, so I asked God for a picture of the Holy Spirit. I was quite surprised when He gave me a picture of Jesus. I remembered that Scripture says the Holy Spirit did not speak in His own authority (John 16:13). It also said, "He will bring me (Jesus) glory by telling you whatever he receives from me" (John 16:14 NLT).

The Holy Spirit points the way to Jesus. He draws people to Jesus and not to Himself (John16:13-14). Jesus did not take glory for Himself either, but pointed the way to His Father: "The words I speak are not my own, but my Father who lives in me does his work through me" (John 14:10 NLT). Jesus lived in dependence on His Father when He walked the earth. He prayed to His Father and talked to Him. He gave Him honor and glory. The Holy Spirit points us to Jesus and Jesus, in turn, points the way to the Father.

When I begin my prayer time, I will usually start by saying, "Holy Spirit, please show me what is on the Father's heart for this situation today." When I read the Bible, I say, "Holy Spirit, please open the Word to me and bring revelation about the Scriptures." Even though He doesn't draw the attention to Himself, we see and experience Him more if we acknowledge His presence and His help. It is like acknowledging the presence of a friend.

Years ago when I was struggling a lot, I asked God what the purpose of life was. He answered me from Colossians, "And this is the secret: that Christ in your hearts is your only hope of glory" (Colossians 1:27 TLB), and "so you have everything when you have Christ" (Colossians 2:10 TLB). It was one of those questions to which

I hadn't expected an answer, but God answered me through my Bible reading. When we keep our focus on Jesus, we keep perspective. When our eyes start wandering to the problems or concerns or troubles and they becomes the main focus, we go down a winding downward spiral of feeling discouraged, hopeless, and depressed. The Bible and prayer bring our lives back into focus; they center us and return us to God's perspective.

During a time of financial struggle I saw photos of the joyful smiling faces of orphans at a ministry in Africa. We have so much more than they do, but look at their joy. In the western world our joy is often connected to our circumstances and finances. As we get to the place where we find our joy in our relationship with God and experience the communion of the Holy Spirit, we walk in a much higher place.

I once heard a ministry leader speak who was always very excited about God. I knew he faced challenges, and I wondered how he managed to continue to be excited about God in the midst of challenges. That day he shared how he kept his focus on Jesus and on beholding God. He said he went outside at night and looked at the stars and said, "God, You made all the stars and You love me." He was in such awe that it helped him trust God about everything else. If we can keep that childlike focus on God, no matter what happens we will run the race with endurance. We have a choice—we can allow circumstances to pull us down or we can keep our eyes on Jesus, "looking unto Jesus, the author and finisher of our faith" (Hebrews 12:2).

"Salvation is a gift, but spiritual maturity is attained through a gradual process of spiritual growth. This process begins at the time of our spiritual birth, and is comparable to the stages of our natural growth."[22] We know that babies are dependent on their parents for all their needs. With proper care a baby becomes a child, then a teenager, and eventually becomes an independent young adult. As spiritual babies, we need the right care and spiritual food to grow.

Just as there are seasons in nature, we go through different seasons too. Just after we have given our lives to Jesus, we are in a season of

---

22. Wade E. Taylor, *Waterspouts of Glory, Volume One*, (Greensboro, NC: Wade Taylor Publications, 1995), 73.

great joy and we see God's provision and miracles. Then we come into a season where God doesn't always answer every prayer the way we want. He is teaching us to walk in faith. We even go through challenging winter seasons, times when we feel God is pruning us and cutting us back. "The *'winter'* represents a time of *'barrenness'* in our spiritual experience, during which the Lord is seemingly absent from us, and in which there is little or no quickening of His presence within us, or our ministry. The winter season is the time in which the Lord removes the old to make room for the new."[23]

In our walk with God He takes us through many different experiences. "These experiences that result from His indwelling life do not come simply through any intellectual comprehension or understanding of His Word. Rather, they require the impartation of His life to us, as we fellowship (sup) with Him. Only then can there be any impartation of *'spirit and life'* to others. We cannot give that which we do not first possess."[24] We can learn knowledge and teach it to others, but when knowledge becomes experiential, it becomes wisdom and can impart life. "Yes, I am the vine; you are the branches. Those who remain in me, and I in them, will produce much fruit. For apart from me you can do nothing" (John 15:5 NLT).

Spiritual Disciplines

We need both the Spirit and the Word to grow and mature, and spiritual disciplines prepare room for the Holy Spirit to have His way. The Word establishes the foundation and the Spirit brings life. Spiritual disciplines provide the foundation for the Holy Spirit to take what we learned and use it. Spiritual disciplines help us grow in our relationship with the Lord. We are going to look at reading the Bible, praying, waiting on the Lord and worship. If we do not know the Bible, it is easy to be deceived. When I ask the Holy Spirit for a word for someone, often a Scripture comes to mind. Even if I don't remember the whole Scripture, I often remember where to find it in the Bible. He can give us words of wisdom, encouragement, or discernment. Sometimes as I go about

---
23. Ibid., 84.
24. Ibid., 86.

my daily tasks, I will suddenly think about a situation and immediately know how to pray for it. This is the exact right time to pray. If I wait until later, I find that I have forgotten what the situation or the prayer was. Any word from the Holy Spirit will have an impact. He knows exactly the right time, so you cannot go wrong when He leads you. Often it happens very naturally. It is powerful to proclaim Scripture or blessings or truth over our children or people we know. When we speak Holy Spirit-inspired truth, we release that flow.

Reading the Word

It is essential to read the Bible for ourselves. We will not spiritually survive if we only go to church once a week and don't personally cultivate a relationship with God through regular Bible reading and prayer. Reading the Bible pulls me back to the truth. It aligns my life. It keeps the truth before me, and I need that desperately, more than I am even aware.

When I was a young Christian, I sat under the teaching of a woman who spent hours studying her Bible every day; her teaching was life giving. Her influence caused me to desire to receive revelation from the Holy Spirit when I read the Bible too. I prayed before I read the Bible: "Holy Spirit, please open the Word to me, bring understanding, and speak to me."

It is helpful to talk to God about what we read in the Bible and ask Him questions. It delights His heart to show you His truth. Listen to the Holy Spirit. Sometimes I get a sense from Him that I should read a Scripture in a different translation or look up a word in the Greek or Hebrew. Some Scriptures can be turned into prayers, and then I pray them, thus: "Father, give me boldness in sharing Your Word. Create in me a clean heart, O God, and renew a steadfast spirit within me" (Acts 4:38; Psalm 51:10).

Some people prefer to read the Bible from cover to cover; others like to focus on a specific chapter at a time. God has met me in both ways, sometimes surprising me in my routine reading as I pick up where I left off the previous day, and other times by stirring me to read a chapter or certain book of the Bible that was not part of my routine.

Discovering the Holy Spirit

Praying

Prayer is as easy as talking to God. The Bible tells us to cast our cares upon God (1 Peter 5:7). Carrying those cares won't make them lighter. It is much better to release them daily into God's hands through prayer. If I have a stubborn situation that needs a breakthrough, I often find a Scripture or a one sentence prayer that I can easily remember and pray that daily for the situation.

I pray for my family every day. If I don't pray for them, who will? Their well-being is important to me. Years ago I read in 1 Corinthians 2: "But the spiritual man has insight into everything, and that bothers and baffles the man of the world, who can't understand him at all. How could he? For certainly he has never been one to know the Lord's thoughts, or to discuss them with him, or to move the hands of God by prayer" (1 Corinthians 2:16 TLB).

The last part of the Scripture made an impression on me, "to move the hands of God by prayer." It changed my whole perspective about prayer. I can make a difference in the outcome of things through prayer. It doesn't mean we can manipulate God through prayer. We partner with the Holy Spirit. We hear what is on His heart for a situation and then pray it back to Him. If I just pray my will or wisdom it can work the same as witchcraft, which is controlling prayer. I learned to ask God what He wants me to pray for situations. When I know His will, I am confident and have faith. We can discern His will for many situations from the Bible. I can sense if the Holy Spirit is in a prayer. Sometimes the Holy Spirit will give me a prayer for a situation. I just pray it right there and then if I can, because if I try to do it later I forget the prayer.

Prayers of blessing can be very powerful too. One afternoon our oldest son was on his way out to go to work. As he left, I sensed I should bless him and said, "Jesus, bless, bless, bless you today." He came back that evening and said it was his best night of tips he had ever received. I have prayed blessings without that impact, but I really felt that God wanted to bless my son that night. I felt the presence of the Holy Spirit on the blessing. God wanted me to speak it and the words released what God wanted to do. When we partner with the Holy Spirit to release His words, they change situations. I don't miss an opportunity to bless someone when I can. God asked the Israelites to choose, "I call heaven and earth as witnesses today against you, that I have set before you life and death, blessing and cursing; therefore choose life, that both you and your descendants may live" (Deuteronomy 30:19).

Living in obedience to God and focusing on loving God can cut out quite a bit of warfare, but there are seasons when things in the spirit get stirred up. We have authority to bind the work of the enemy when he comes against our families, finances, etc. (Matthew 18:18). A lady who spoke at a women's breakfast mentioned that she had to take authority over the enemy daily, cancelling every assignment of the enemy over the life of one of her children. It was just a time when the enemy was coming against the plans God had for that child. This helped me. We have authority to cancel the plans of the enemy. Thank You, Jesus!

During times of warfare I try to discern how the Holy Spirit wants me to respond. There were times when I felt I should take authority and other times when He said, *sit still and God will fight for you*. Responding in the opposite spirit is a type of warfare too. When someone doesn't treat you well, pray blessings over them. Every time a negative thought or emotion comes, turn it into a blessing. Stop every negative thought as soon as it comes to you and turn it into a positive prayer. If you have a fearful thought about the safety of you children, pray like this, "Father I bless my children today. They are Your children. Release angels to encamp around them, protect and help them. I bless them to love and know You, Lord."

I have prayed this Scripture for my children for many years: "As for me, this is my promise to them; says the Lord: 'My Holy Spirit shall not leave them, and they shall want the good and hate the wrong—they and their children and their children's children forever'" (Isaiah 59:21 TLB). In times when I have been very involved with intercession and felt the warfare pick up, I often prayed that God would hide me in Jesus. "For you died, and your life is hidden with Christ in God" (Colossians 3:3).

Waiting on the Lord

This is my favorite spiritual discipline—to sit in the presence of God. It can be done with worship music or just in the quiet. In my spirit

I engage with the Holy Spirit, sometimes singing with the worship, other times just being quiet, enjoying His presence. There are times when I focus on a Scripture or just pray. Outwardly it doesn't look like much is happening, but inwardly I am connecting with the Holy Spirit. Many times God just shows up during these times with His still, quiet presence. Then I don't talk. I just sit with Him, content to know that He is near. Often I sit with Jesus for half an hour or more. It might feel like He didn't speak to me or nothing much happened, but later in the day He will speak to me or give me revelation. It brings freedom when you make time to be with Him without an agenda. He can speak to us at any given moment, but He just wants to enjoy your presence so just be there with Him. "He will rejoice over you with gladness, He will quiet you with His love, He will rejoice over you with singing" (Zephaniah 3:17).

One morning I went to the house of prayer and my plan was to write. Usually I read my Bible or sit with Jesus for a while before I start to work. That morning as I tried to write, nothing flowed. I realized writing was not on God's agenda that day, and I spent more time sitting with Him. That was what He wanted me to do that day. I came out of that feeling very fulfilled and at peace even though I didn't actually do anything. The next day I went back to my regular schedule, but I was thankful that I had sensed what God was doing the previous day; otherwise I would have been very frustrated, trying to force my agenda instead.

Worship

Mary poured out the perfume on Jesus' feet and the fragrance filled the room (John 12:3). Worship is like that. God receives worship from a sincere heart like a beautiful fragrance. One day I was surprised by Jonah 1. God told Jonah, "Go to the great city of Nineveh, and give them this announcement from the Lord: 'I am going to destroy you, for your wickedness rises before me; it smells to highest heaven'" (Jonah 1:2 TLB). If wickedness smells bad then righteousness smells good. Imagine what a beautiful smell worship is to God.

Several years ago we had a worship and prayer time in a small chapel. There were about fifteen people there; one was playing guitar.

As we were singing praises to God, my son saw a vision. He saw the worship forming a corkscrew. This swirling light went up. He saw a black net over the city and the worship created a hole in the net. He saw black figures trying to patch up the hole, but beams of light went up and created holes in the net from other places in the city. As he watched, he saw the net tear to such an extent that it was beyond repair. Worship is powerful. The worship of a few people can affect the second heaven where rulers and principalities are (Ephesians 6:12). This encourages my heart to worship even more.

When we give our lives to Jesus, we become citizens of a new kingdom. We become citizens of heaven. *The Message* puts it this way, "So if you're serious about living this new resurrection life with Christ, act like it. Pursue the things over which Christ presides. Don't shuffle along, eyes to the ground, absorbed with the things right in front of you. Look up, and be alert to what is going on around Christ—that's where the action is. See things from His perspective" (Colossians 3:1-3 MSG). Ephesians 2:6 tells us that we are seated in heavenly places. We can see things from God's perspective. He usually has a different perspective on a situation than we do; that is why we should ask Him how to pray.

In John 14-17, Jesus shared some powerful truths with His disciples before He died. John 14:15 says, "If you love Me, keep My commandments." Love will empower us to say no to sin. When we love someone, we don't want to hurt them. I love Jesus; if I do something that hurts Him, I feel that hurt within me. I would much rather feel His joy and peace in my heart. Jesus told them He would not leave them by themselves. He would ask His Father to send them a Helper. This Helper had been with them, but the time would come when He would live inside them: "But you know him already because he has been staying with you, and will even be in you!" (John 14:17 MSG). The Holy Spirit has a direct connection to God, so He can share with us what is on God's heart for us to do and pray. It doesn't mean we throw out our common sense or don't use our minds anymore.

A pastor once explained the Scripture about wives submitting to their husbands. He said his wife had a mind of her own and there were decisions she could make for herself. She didn't have to ask him if she wanted to go and have tea with her friends or go to the grocery store, but when there were bigger decisions that involved both of them or the family, they made those decisions together. The Holy Spirit works very much in the same way. He wants to be involved with our lives. I have a schedule and I try to hear God's voice in setting it up. As I do the things I need to do, the Holy Spirit is right there with me. He can bring someone to mind to pray for as I am driving or walking in the store. He can help me find the best deals. It is wonderful to have a friend I can always share my life with. I have learned to value His input. I do not abdicate my will, but submit mine to God's.

Colossians 3 paints a picture of the clothing we need to wear, "Put on your new nature, and be renewed as you learn to know your Creator and become like him" (Colossians 3:10 NLT). "So, chosen by God for this new life of love, dress in the wardrobe God picked out for you: compassion, kindness, humility, quiet strength, discipline. Be even-tempered, content with second place, quick to forgive an offense. Forgive as quickly and completely as the Master forgave you. And regardless of what else you put on, wear love. It's your basic, all purpose garment. Never be without it" (Colossians 3:12-14 MSG). First John 4 reaffirms this life of love beautifully.

> "My beloved friends, let us continue to love each other since love comes from God. Everyone who loves is born of God and experiences a relationship with God. The person who refuses to love doesn't know the first thing about God, because God is love—so you can't know him if you don't love.
>
> "This is how God showed his love for us: God sent his only Son into the world, so we might live through him. This is the kind of love we are talking about—not that we once upon a time loved God, but that he loved us and sent his Son as a sacrifice to clear away our sins and the damage they've done to our relationship with God.
>
> "My dear, dear friends, if God loved us like this, we certainly ought to love each other. No one has seen God,

ever. But if we love one another, God dwells deeply within us, and his love becomes complete in us—perfect love! This is how we know we're living steadily and deeply in him, and he in us: He's given us life from his life, from his very own Spirit....

God is love. When we take up permanent residence in a life of love, we live in God and God lives in us" (1 John 4:10-13, 17 MSG).

One day we were doing a two-hour "Worship with the Word" prayer and worship session at the house of prayer. The Scriptures that I had selected to pray were about God's love. We started with loving the Lord your God with all your heart (Matthew 22:37). Then we focused on the love Jesus has for us, singing and praying about it—there was no greater love a person could have than what Jesus did by laying down His life (John 15:13). The Song of Solomon 2:4 came to mind and we prayed and sang that His banner over our lives is love. In conclusion, the phrase came to me that He surrounds us with His love and faithfulness. Through our prayer and singing, the Holy Spirit painted a picture of loving God, followed by the way Jesus loved us so much that He gave His life for us. Then He covered us with love—His banner over our lives is love and finally He surrounded us with His love and faithfulness. What a beautiful picture of being safe and secure in God's love. It is a picture of peace, "And let the peace that comes from Christ rule in your hearts. For as members of one body you are called to live in peace" (Colossians 3:15).

There have been times in my life when it felt like God was far away. When Jesus went to the cross He said, "My God, my God, why have You forsaken Me?" (Matthew 27:46). For a small period of time Jesus was separated from His Father. That was so difficult that Jesus sweat blood in the garden before He went to the cross. At a time when it felt like a breakthrough would never come, a friend gave me this word—"this momentary affliction." It was from 2 Corinthians 4:17: "For our light affliction, which is but for a moment, is working for us a far more exceeding and eternal weight of glory." That was not what I wanted to hear.

Discovering the Holy Spirit

In the nearly thirty years that I have been a Christian, I have learned that there are times when God feels really close, and then there are times when we go through trials or testings and He feels far away. The Bible says He will not leave or forsake us (Hebrews 13:5,8), so whether I feel Him or not, He is with me. I have to live by faith and not by what I feel. It is wonderful though when, after a time of testing, He comes close again.

In this journey called life you have a Father in heaven, who is the best Daddy you will ever know. You have a Brother and Friend, Jesus, who gave everything for you, to rescue you from hell. Then you have a Helper and best Friend, the Holy Spirit, who will never leave you and who lives in you: "for in Him we live and move and have our being" (Acts 17:28). The Bible says Enoch walked in habitual fellowship with God and was pleasing and satisfactory to Him (Genesis 5:24 and Hebrews 11:5 AMP). Abraham was called a friend of God (James 2:23). That is the invitation that we have—to walk habitually with God and live a life that is pleasing to Him. You have been invited into the most exciting relationship in the universe. I see a picture of a man on one knee, asking a woman for her hand in marriage. This is what Jesus is offering you—to be part of the marriage supper of the Lamb (Revelation 19:7-9). The invitation is not for a relationship at some time in the future; it is for now—every day every moment. The only thing He wants is a willing heart that says, "Yes!"

Hermie Reynolds

Discussion Questions: Growing in the Holy Spirit

1. Read the following Scriptures; they all contain the word *wait*: Isaiah 40:31, Psalm 27:14, and Psalm 37:7. What do you learn from these Scriptures?

   _____
   _____
   _____
   _____
   _____

2. Share what you can do to increase your joy and peace in Jesus.

   _____
   _____
   _____
   _____
   _____

3. Write down a description of who the Holy Spirit is. Then turn back to the questions for chapter one and read what you wrote there. Discuss how you have grown in this journey in getting to know the Holy Spirit.

   _____
   _____
   _____
   _____
   _____
   _____
   _____

Discovering the Holy Spirit

4. Read the verse below; underline and discuss the parts of the prayer that speak to you. Read it in your own Bible too. You can use what the Holy Spirit highlights to you as a personal prayer for you or your family.

> "Asking God to give you wise minds and spirits attuned to his will, and so acquire a thorough understanding of the ways in which God works. We pray that you'll live well for the Master, making him proud of you as you work hard in his orchard. As you learn more and more how God works, you will learn how to do your work. We pray that you'll have the strength to stick it out over the long haul—not the grim strength of gritting your teeth but the glory-strength God gives. It is strength that endures the unendurable and spills over into joy" (Colossians 1:9-11 MSG).

_____
_____
_____
_____
_____
_____
_____

5. Read Romans 12:1-3. Read it in your own Bible and read *The Message* version too. Spend some time thinking and praying about these ideas. Ask the Holy Spirit to show you if there are any areas that you think too much like our culture and not like Jesus.

> "So here's what I want you to do, God helping you: Take your everyday, ordinary—your sleeping, eating, going-to-work, and walking around life—and place it before God as an offering. Embracing what God does for you is the best thing you can do for him. Don't become so well-adjusted to your culture that you fit into it without even thinking. Instead fix your attention on God. You'll be changed from

the inside out. Readily recognize what he wants from you, and quickly respond to it. Unlike the culture around you, always dragging you down to its level of immaturity, God brings the best out of you, develops well-formed maturity in you" (Romans 12:1-3).

About the Author

Hermie Reynolds and her husband, John, live in Hamilton, Ohio, and have four grown children. She taught in a public school until she had children, and then she and her husband led the children's ministry in their church in South Africa for ten years. In 1999, they moved to Cincinnati, Ohio. She has since taught many classes about the attributes of God, and prayed for the Cincinnati region for more than ten years, at the Cincinnati House of Prayer. John and Hermie are part of the Oxford Vineyard Church planting team. Hermie is the author of *Discovering God* and *Discovering Jesus*.

Hermie can be contacted at hermiereynolds@gmail.com or visit www.DiscoveringGod.info.

More Titles by Hermie Reynolds

Discovering God
by Hermie Reynolds
$14.95
ISBN: 978-1-936578-73-3

Discovering God by Hermie Reynolds answers some of the questions that people ask every day such as: Who is God? Is God good? Can He be trusted? Does He care about me? We live in a time where we see natural disasters like never before. These things cause us to ask questions. These questions and their biblical answers are addressed in this book. Hermie shows how a personal and intimate relationship with Him is the most exciting and meaningful relationship someone will ever have and can help people navigate through the questions.

Discovering God by Hermie Reynolds will bring greater understanding about the way God works. It is designed to be used individually or in small groups. Each chapter has discussion questions which will help those reading to dig deeper into the Scriptures and apply what they have learned to their life and situation.

More Titles by Hermie Reynolds

Discovering Jesus
by Hermie Reynolds
$14.95
ISBN: 978-1-936578-98-6

Discovering Jesus by Hermie Reynolds is a straightforward book about Jesus written for both believer and unbeliever alike who want to understand who Jesus is better. Jesus walked on the earth over two thousand years ago. His story made it around the world and into the movie theaters. *Discovering Jesus* will take you on a journey from the Old Testament to the birth of Jesus, His ministry on earth and His death on the cross. Yet it did not end there; He rose again and appeared to many until He ascended into heaven. One day He will return as Bridegroom King. Hermie shows that He is worth spending the time to find out who He was and is and why He paid such a great price for you and me.

Discovering Jesus by Hermie Reynolds is written in an easy-to-read style with Bible stories, Scriptures, and examples of how God worked in the lives of Hermie and her family in order to draw them closer to Jesus. Ideal for individual use or small groups, each chapter has discussion questions and Scripture references that make it possible to go deeper into the Bible to help you grow in your relationship with Jesus.

www.ingramcontent.com/pod-product-compliance
Lightning Source LLC
Chambersburg PA
CBHW050534300426
44113CB00012B/2100